Thank you for your faithful
support this past year.

Merry Christmas!
ೞ
From The Staff of
Long Island Youth For Christ

December 2013

THE NATIVITY COLLECTION

by Robert J. Morgan

THOMAS NELSON
Since 1978

NASHVILLE   DALLAS   MEXICO CITY   RIO DE JANEIRO   BEIJING

Published in Nashville, Tennessee, by Thomas Nelson. Thomas Nelson is a registered trademark of Thomas Nelson, Inc.

Thomas Nelson, Inc., titles may be purchased in bulk for educational, business, fund-raising, or sales promotional use. For information, please e-mail SpecialMarkets@ ThomasNelson.com.

Project Manager: Lisa Stilwell

Cover and interior design by Koechel Peterson Design, Minneapolis, MN

Scripture quotations are taken from THE NEW KING JAMES VERSION. © 1982, 1992 by Thomas Nelson, Inc. Used by permission. All rights reserved. HOLY BIBLE: NEW INTERNATIONAL VERSION® (niv). © 1973, 1978, 1984 by International Bible Society. Used by permission of Zondervan Publishing House. All rights reserved.

ISBN-13: 978-1-4041-8974-4

Printed in Singapore

10 11 12 13 14 [TWP] 5 4 3 2 1

DEDICATED TO LILLIAN RUTH

Table of Contents

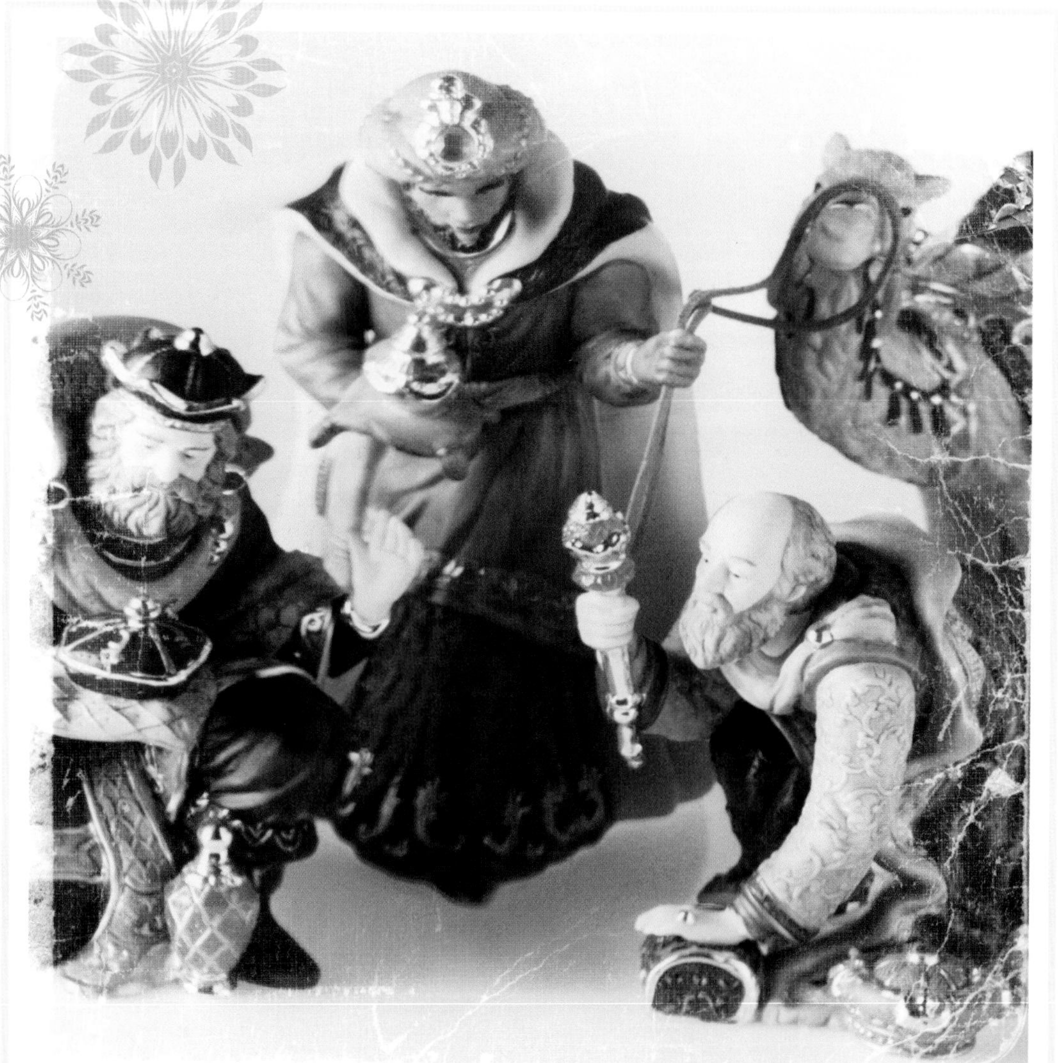

Foreword

 have always loved stories. I love to read them, and I love to tell them. I cannot preach without them and—according to my wife—I cannot carry on a conversation without them.

Life is one story made up of many stories . . . the story of our childhood and of our youth . . . the story of our marriage and of the birth of our children . . . the story of our old age and, yes, even the story of our death.

There is something about Christmas that adds to the mystery of stories. I think it has to do with the story of Christmas itself. Could any connected narration of events be as compelling and awe-inspiring as the original, the one found within the pages of the Scriptures?

I believe it is that story that inspires so many other stories at Christmastime. Even those who may not know anything about the story of Christ's birth seem to get caught up in storytelling during the latter days of December.

The late pastor and writer J. B. Phillips has written:

> *If words are to enter men's minds and bear fruit, they must be the right words shaped cunningly to pass men's defenses and explode silently and effectually within their minds.*

Few people I know have the creativity to shape words like that, but my friend Rob Morgan does. When I read his new collection of Christmas stories, I thought of the blessing they must be to the people who hear them for the first time. Each Christmas Eve, Rob reads a brand-new Christmas story to his congregation at the Donelson Fellowship in Nashville. From what I hear, the congregation considers this one of the highlights of the year.

Rob, it's time you let us in on this Christmas blessing.

—*David Jeremiah*

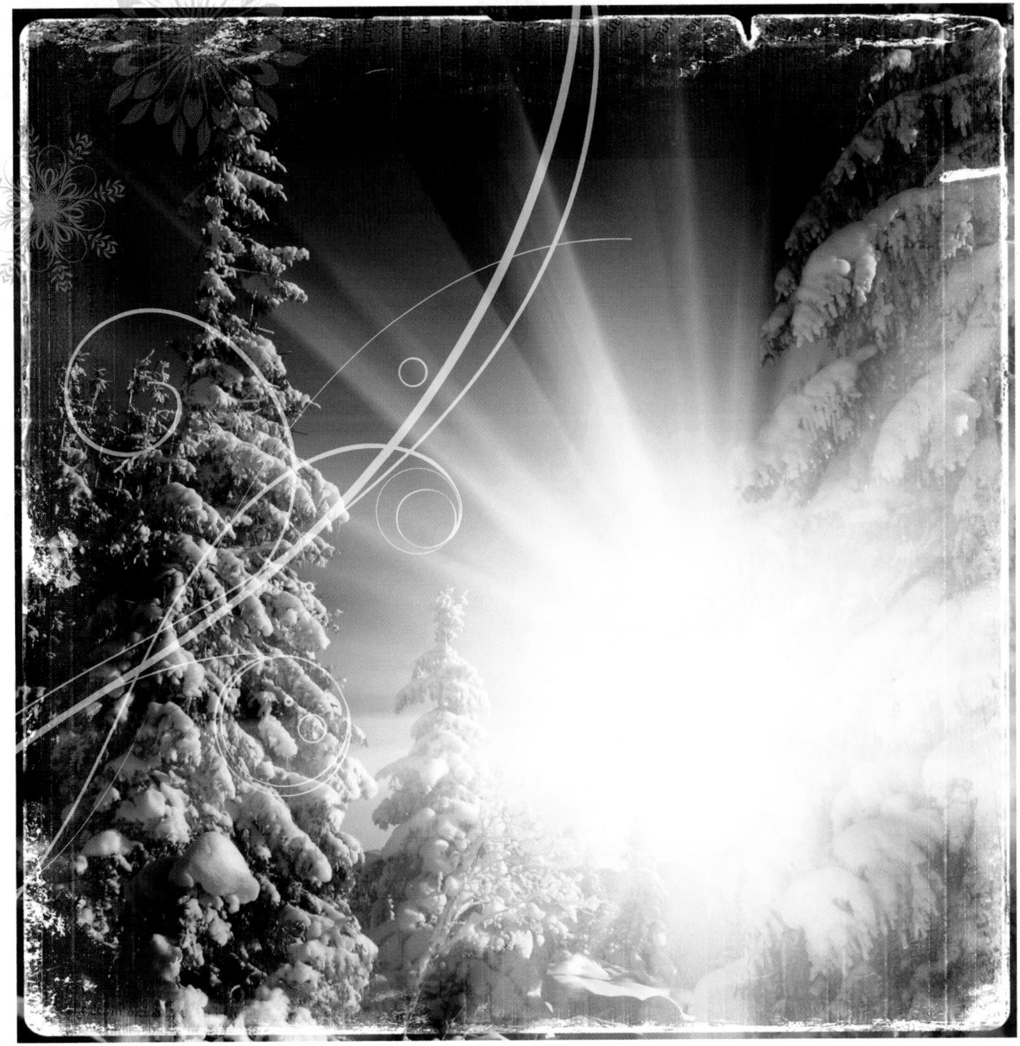

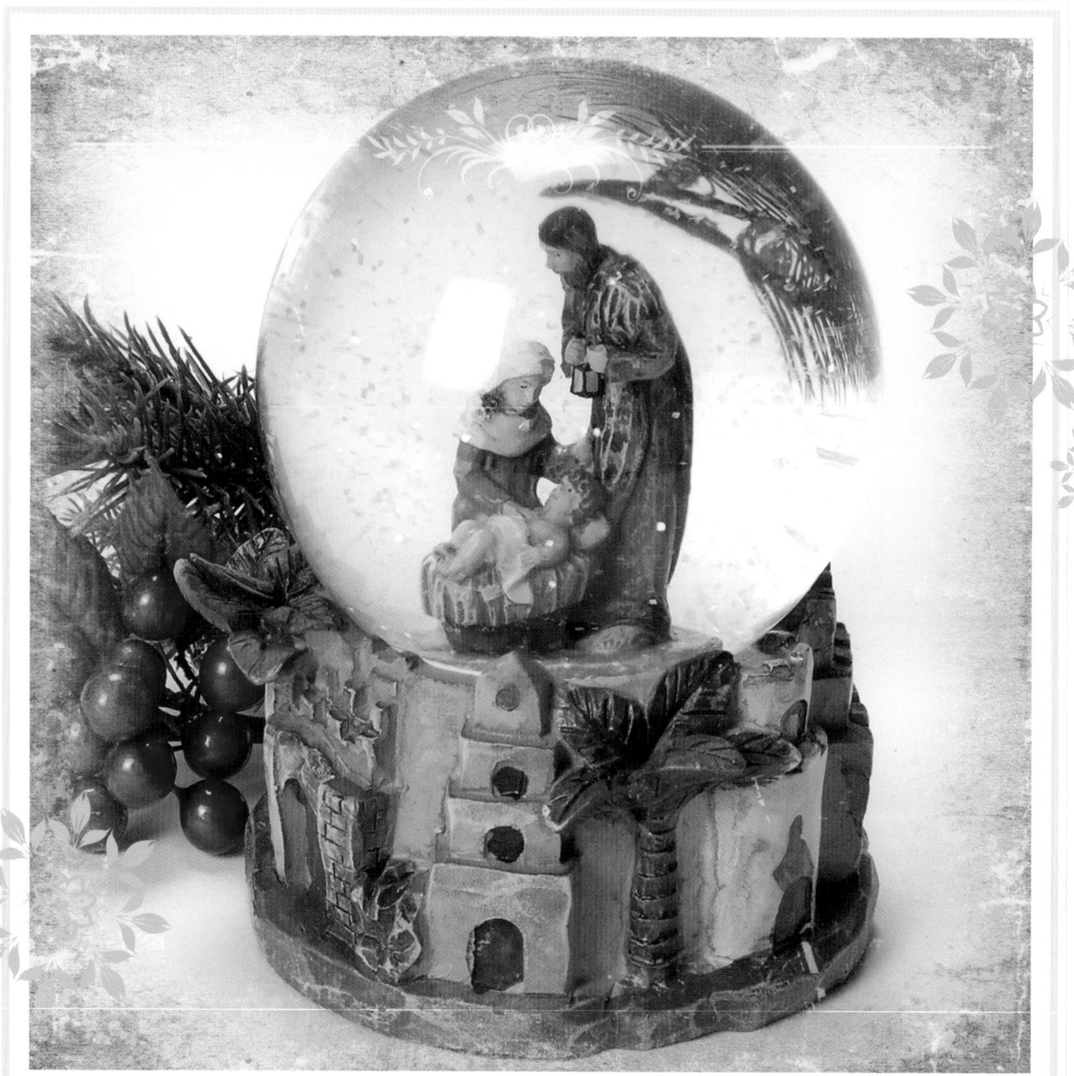

Ollie

I am going to tell you a story, just as my father told it to me, for I can still remember almost word-for-word how he related it to me on Christmas Eve of 1963. We had finished dinner, opened some presents, and put on our pajamas. Just before bedtime, as the last log was burning in the fireplace, I saw my dad walk over to the mantel. He took down the antique snow globe with its small nativity scene and turned the crank on the bottom. The little music box played "Silent Night" as the snow swirled around Joseph, Mary, and the baby in the manger. My dad was lost in thought until the music ceased, then he turned and saw me watching him. I guess I looked at him quizzically, because he went on to recite a little poem I'd never heard before, as though he were explaining something to me.

Silent, holy, calm, and bright,

Jesus came to pierce the night.

Jesus came to make things right.

So be . . .

Silent, holy, calm, and bright,

. . . tonight.

I didn't know what to make of it, so I did what most twelve-year-olds would do. I asked questions. "What d'ya mean, Dad? Where'd you get that old globe, anyhow? Where'd it come from?"

Well, he sat right down in the floor, there in front of the fireplace with the snow globe resting in his lap, and he motioned for me. I sat down beside him, and he turned the thing over and showed me what was stamped on the bottom: *Made in Germany, 1938.* Then he put his arm around me, and this is what he said:

❄ ❄ ❄

Something interesting happened to me, son, when I was your age, when I was twelve years old. It was in 1942. We were living in a little town called Evergreen, Pennsylvania, where my dad had a law practice. Well, that year was unusually busy, and my folks waited until the last possible day—December 24th—to do gift buying. It was about midmorning when we drove downtown, plunged into the crowds on Main Street, and did all

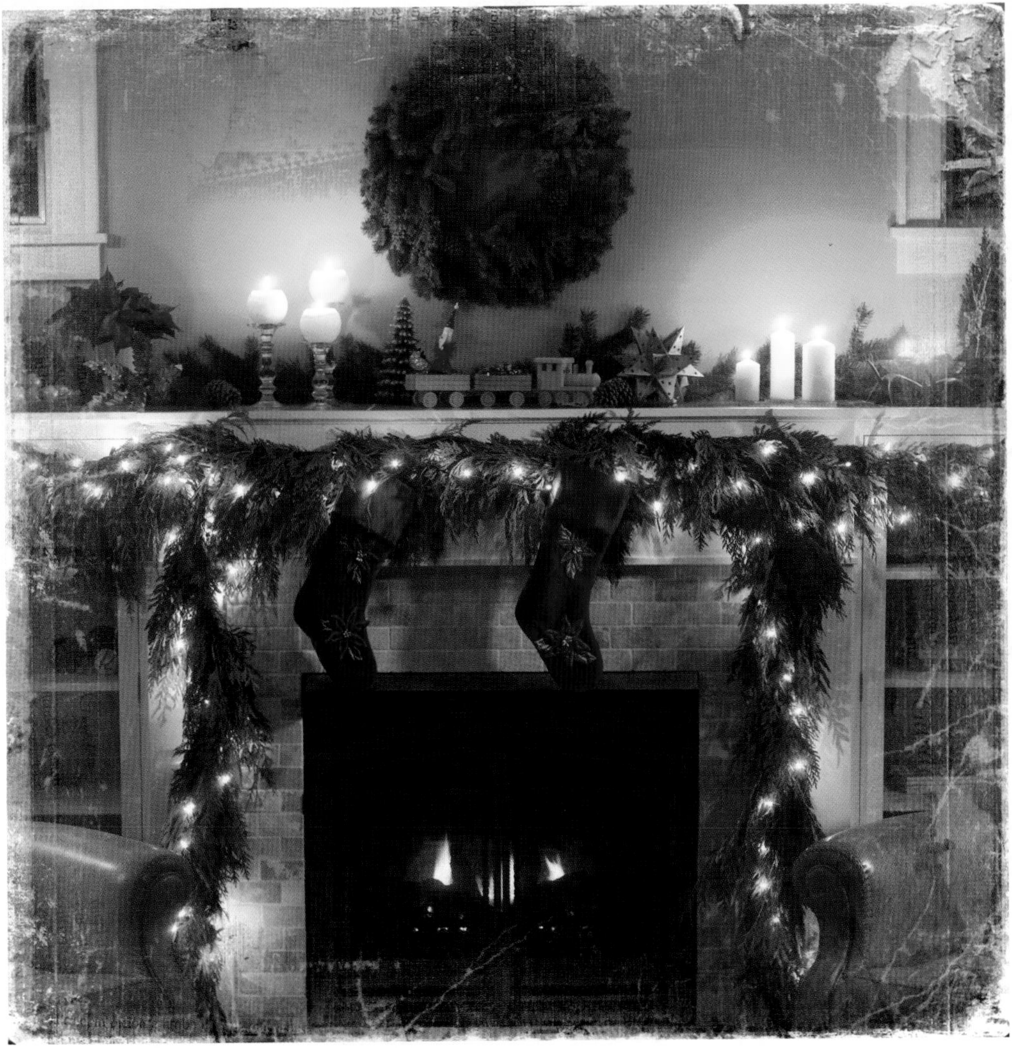

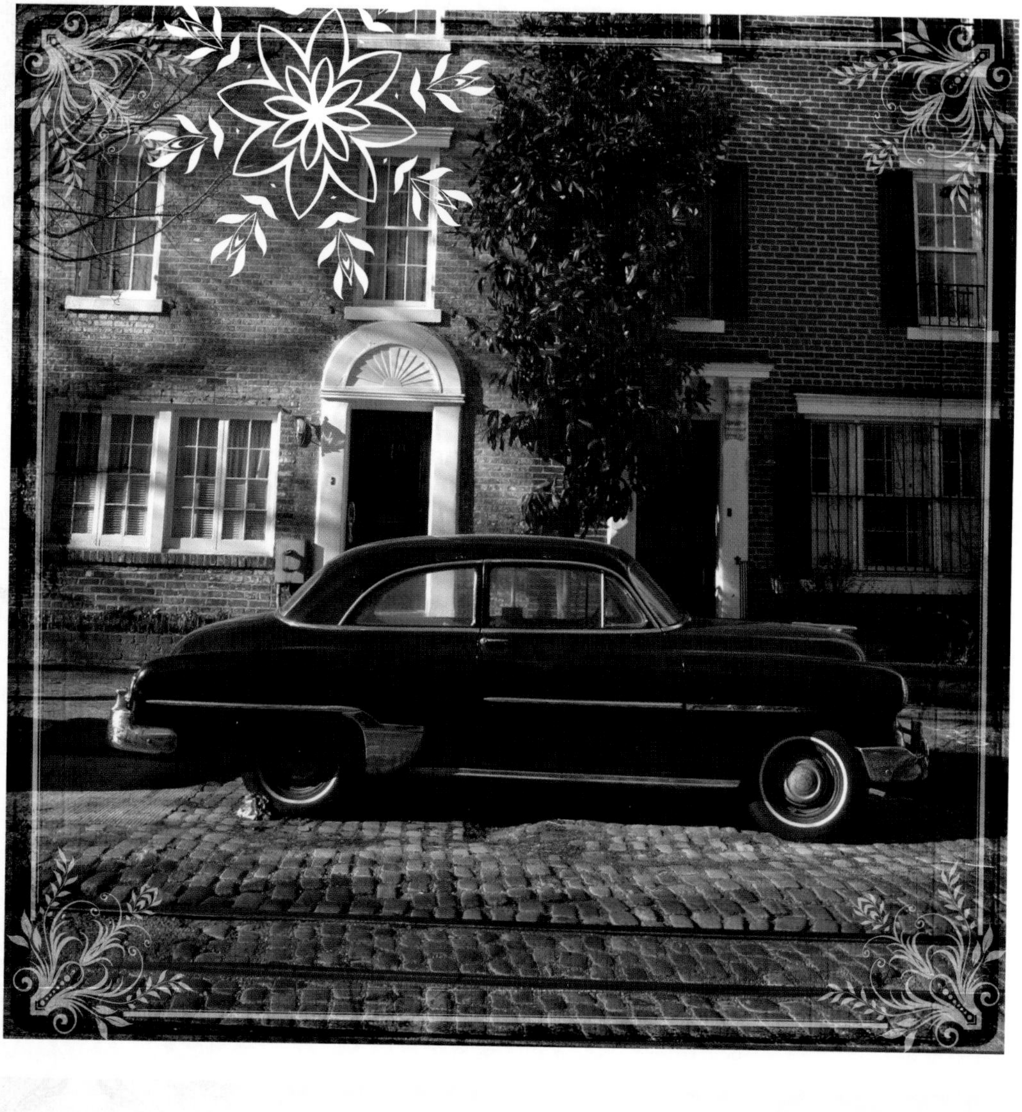

our shopping in one giant trip. Of course, there wasn't much shopping to do back then. World War II was going on, and things were hard to come by. That year we just bought a few items for each other. My dad found a simple necklace for Mom; she bought him a tie and pair of socks; and, from the size of the package, I suspicioned that my gift was a new pair of shoes. We also found a red sweater for my grandma.

We loaded those gifts into the trunk of our 1938 Buick, which we'd left in the town parking lot. Then we walked back to the corner market where we managed to find everything we needed for Christmas Dinner— a canned ham (the only kind available in those days), some cloves and spices, baking potatoes, beans, and carrots. And then some flour, butter, eggs, sugar, and chocolate for a cake. I remember how relieved my mother was to find some of those staples—they were rationed because of the war, you see. After loading everything in the car, we walked down the street one more time and ate a late lunch at the Evergreen Café.

You can imagine our surprise when we returned to the parking lot an hour later and could not find our car. It was gone, vanished, along with our presents and all our food. Someone had stolen our vehicle—and with it they had taken our Christmas. We spent the afternoon in the police station filling out reports, talking to the officers, and listening while they issued bulletins. But it was useless. No one had a clue what had happened to our Buick. My folks were very distressed. The officers said they'd drive us home, but we said we'd just as soon walk as we only lived a few blocks away. By then it was late on the afternoon of Christmas Eve, and the snow was flurrying. So down the street we started, wondering how we were going to celebrate Christmas with no presents and no dinner. Most of the stores had closed, and the shoppers had gone home. We passed the parking lot, and it was empty—almost.

There to our amazement sat our car.

It was on the opposite side of the parking lot. My parents looked at each other in confusion, and we all said things like, "Are we losing our minds?" "Did we forget where we parked?" "I'm sure we parked over here." "Who moved our car over there?"

We walked over to investigate. At first glance it appeared that whoever had moved our car had also washed and cleaned it, for it looked newer and neater than before. But the thief had also cleaned out all our gifts because when my dad opened the trunk, it was empty. We unlocked the doors, got in, and sat there like we were in a fog.

Finally my mom said, "Thomas, this is not our car."

"No," said my dad. "It isn't, is it? But it looks like it." He turned the key in the ignition, and the engine started.

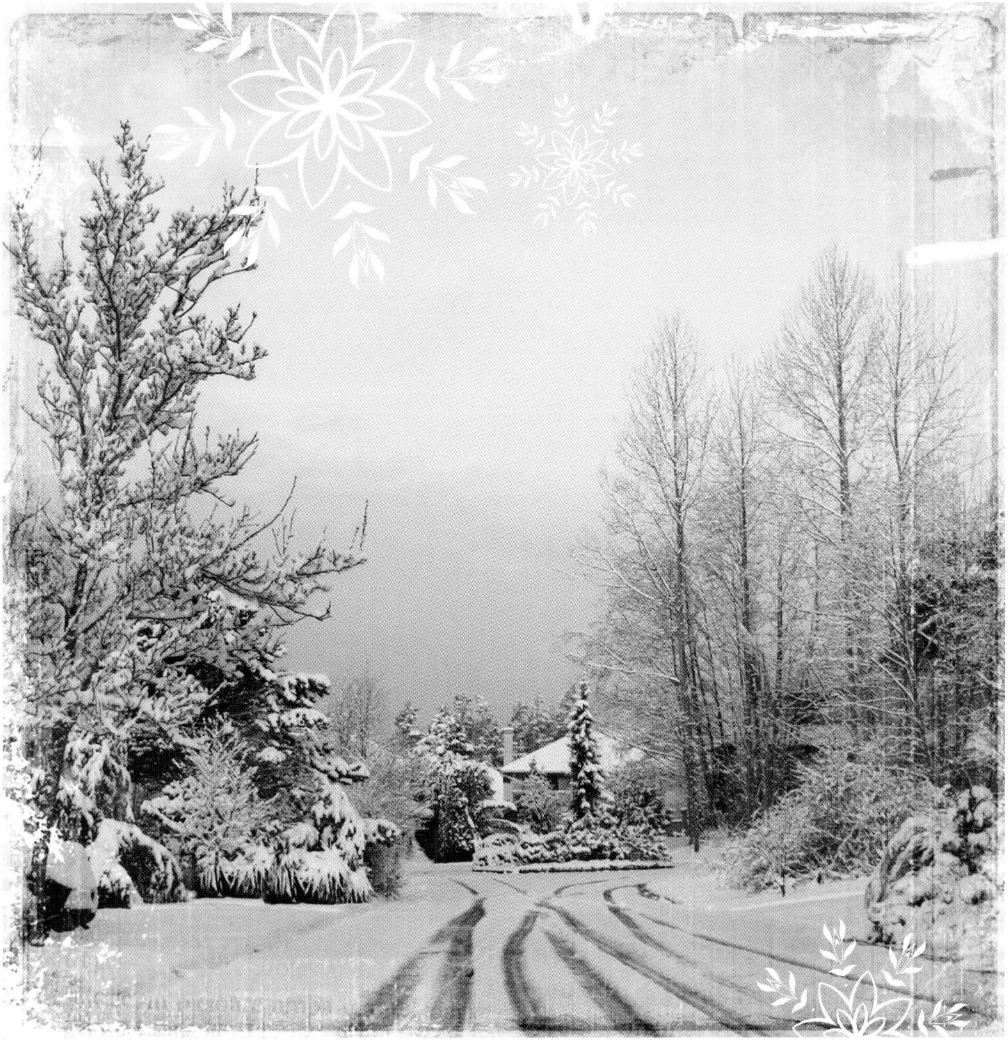

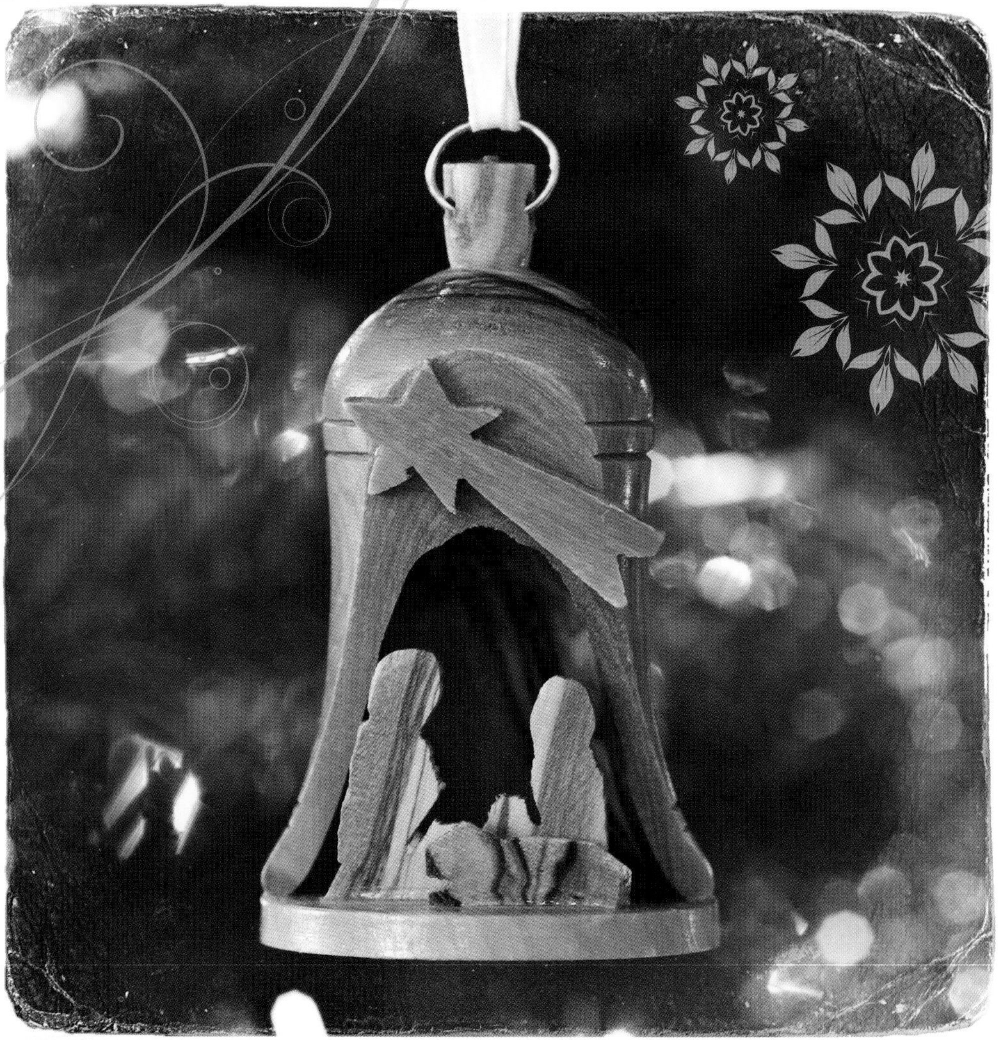

Well, in those days the Detroit carmakers had a limited number of keys and locks, and they were often interchangeable. I remember once my mother locked her keys in the car at school. Another teacher said, "I own a Buick too. Let's see if my key fits your car." And it did. So that explained why the key worked, but it explained nothing else.

My mom opened the glove compartment and found the registration. She said, "This car belongs to Alfreda Reinhart, 508 Elm Street."

"I know her," said my dad. "Well, at least I met her once. I think she's a bit daft. You know, not all there. Do you suppose she could have driven off in our car by mistake?"

"Well, I don't know," said Mom. "I heard some ladies talking about her. It's a sad story. Alfreda is quite elderly. When she lived in Germany, her family was thrown into jail for opposing the National Socialists. She had a son, a daughter-in-law, and a little grandson, a boy of about twelve or so. Some kind of disease swept through the jail, and the whole family died, except Alfreda. After she was released, she managed to leave Germany. Then she moved here to Evergreen where her sister lived, over near the German Lutheran Church. When her sister died, Alfreda seemed to go senile. At least, that's what they said in the beauty shop."

"Yes, and as I recall, she's as deaf as a doornail," said my dad. "And I guess that would explain things. Our cars look alike, the keys are interchangeable, and she must have gotten in the wrong one by mistake. Let's go see."

Well, this was turning into an exciting Christmas for me—a stolen car, an imprisoned family, a crazy old woman, and all our Christmas presents hanging in the balance. It was an adventure!

So off we drove; and ten minutes later we pulled into the driveway at 508 Elm Street. There was our car, all right, sitting in Mrs. Reinhart's carport. We got out and peered in the car windows and opened the trunk. It was empty.

We rang the doorbell, and presently a little hunched lady opened the door. Her hair was thin, white, and disheveled, which was also a description of her. An old pair of glasses sat crookedly on her nose. She wore a faded blue sweater. On seeing us, she burst into joyous smiles. "*Guten Abend*," she cried. "*Guten Abend!* Come in out of the cold! Come in out of the snow! Right on time you are, right on time!"

We stepped into the house. It was rather dark and drafty, but a small fire was burning in the hearth and a little tree sat in the corner. Underneath it were some presents that looked very much like the ones we had bought earlier in the day. I also got a whiff of supper. It smelled like ham with cloves, along with potatoes, carrots, beans, and cake.

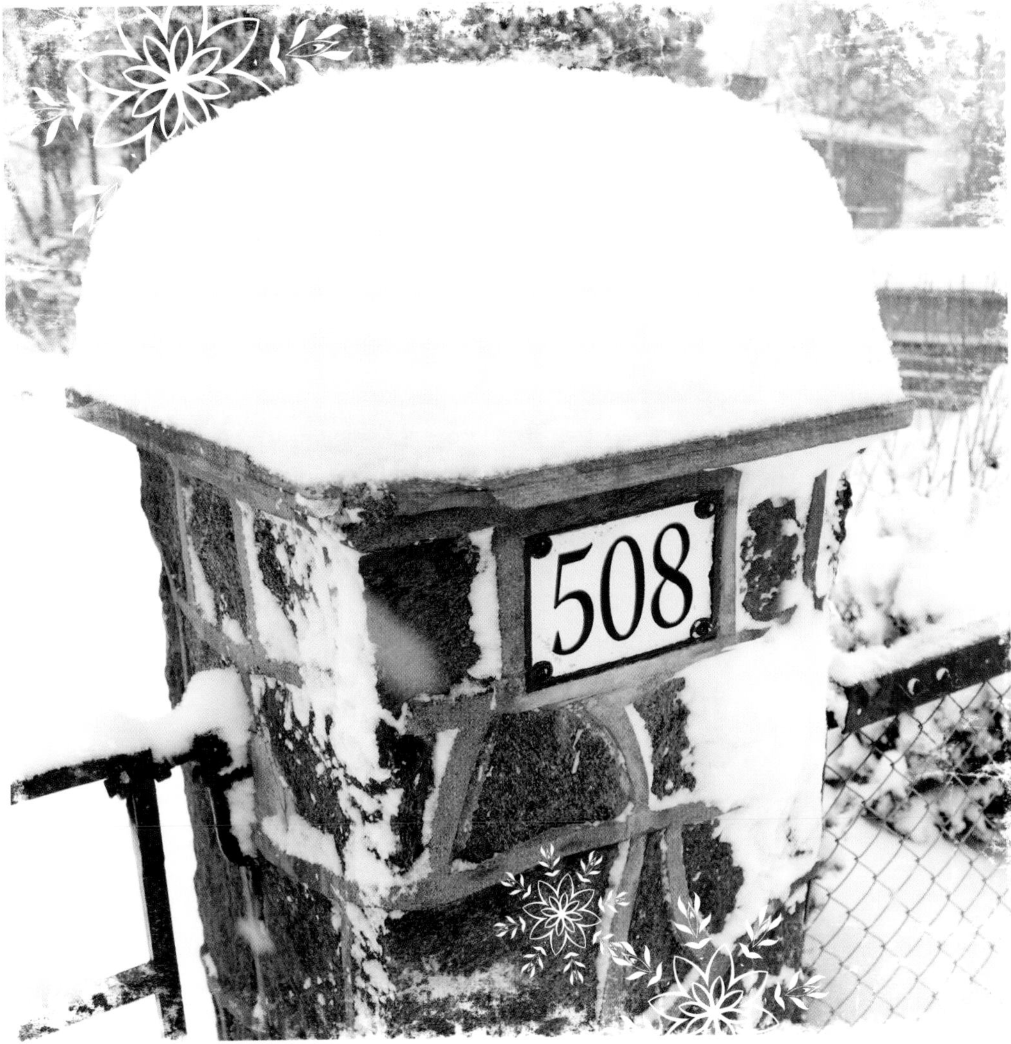
508

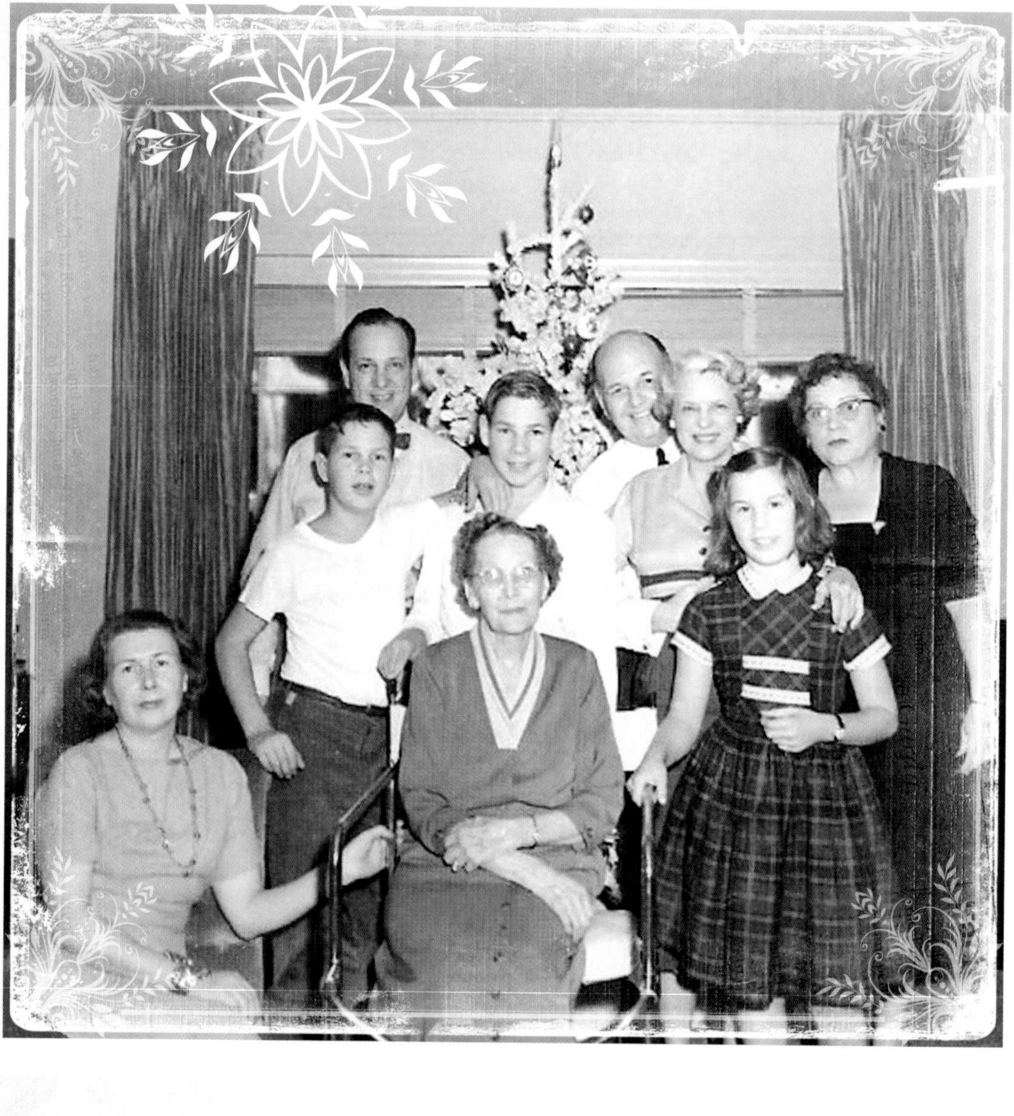

On the mantle was a snow globe, nestled among some garland. I took it all in with a glance.

"Now, give me your coat Gunther, and you, too, Elke," said the old woman. "Oh, how vonderful to see you."

"Frau Reinhart," said my dad, clearing his throat, "I've come to tell you we've mixed up our cars."

Mrs. Reinhart seemed to have trouble understanding, so my dad repeated himself. "We've mixed up our cars."

She looked perplexed. "Vas?" she said.

"Our cars!" said Dad.

"Cigars? Ja, I have cigars. Would you like one?"

"No, no," said my father quickly.

"You always liked your cigars, Gunther," the woman said, shaking her head with a smile. "I try to keep them for you. But for after supper, not before, ja?"

"No, no," said Dad. "What I mean is I think there's been some kind of mistake."

"Ja, of course I have cake too," she said.

"No, no, Frau Reinhart," said my dad, trying a third time, "I'm afraid you're confused. My name is Vicker. Thomas Vicker."

Something about that seemed to distress the old woman. Alfreda Reinhart stared at my dad incredulously, a haunting look on her face, as if trying to comprehend. For some reason, we all sort of stopped breathing for a moment.

"*Nein*," she said.

Again my father said, "Frau Reinhart, my name is Thomas Vicker. Vicker."

"*Nein*, I have no liquor," she said. "I have cigars and cake, but no liquor. Only eggnog." My dad was too flabbergasted to reply, but the atmosphere changed suddenly when the old woman smiled, showing yellow unkempt teeth. "*Sehr gut*," she said, "Your coats. *Bitten*. It's warm in here. Let me help your coats. I've vaited so long for you to get here. I've vaited all afternoon. You're going to stay, aren't you? Of course you are. You've come so far."

She started tugging at sleeves, and I noticed how my parents looked at each other and seemed to reach a kind of understanding. At any rate, they nodded to me, and we all unbuttoned our coats.

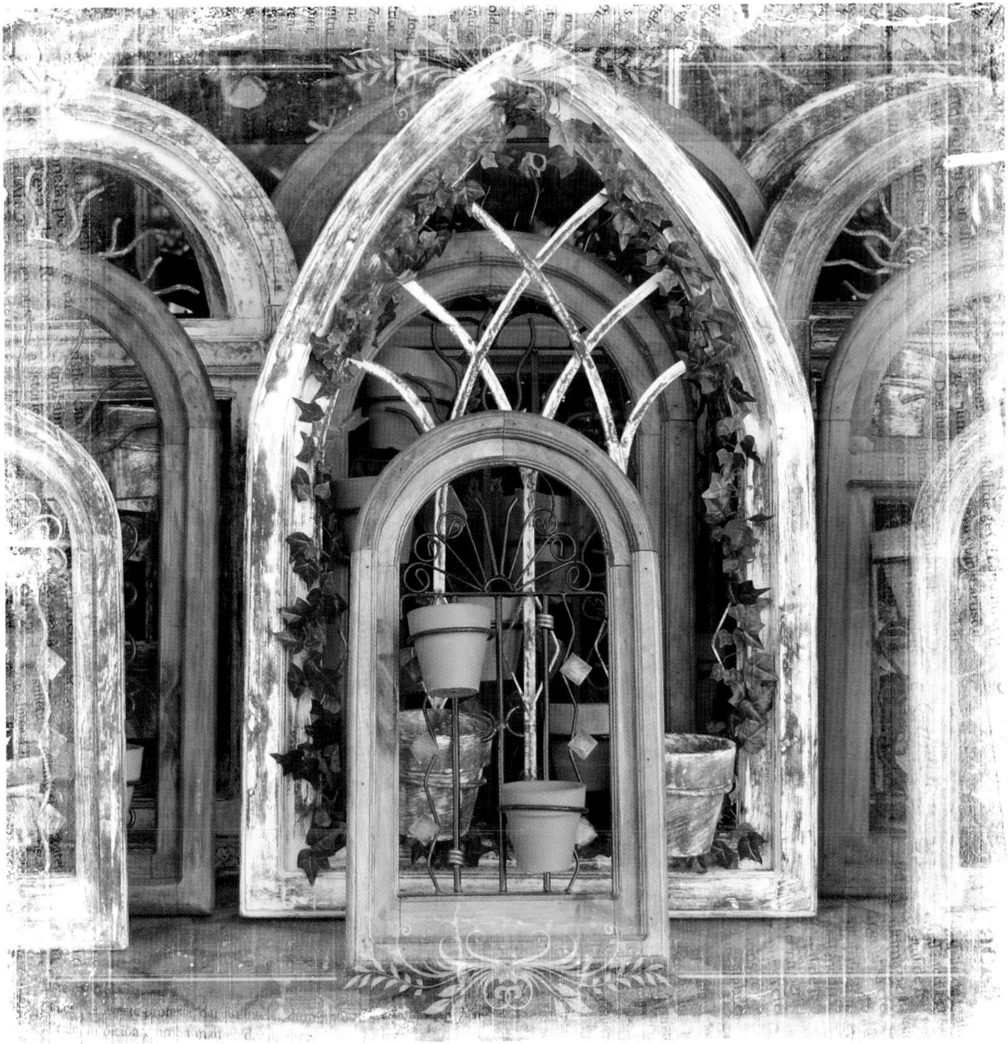

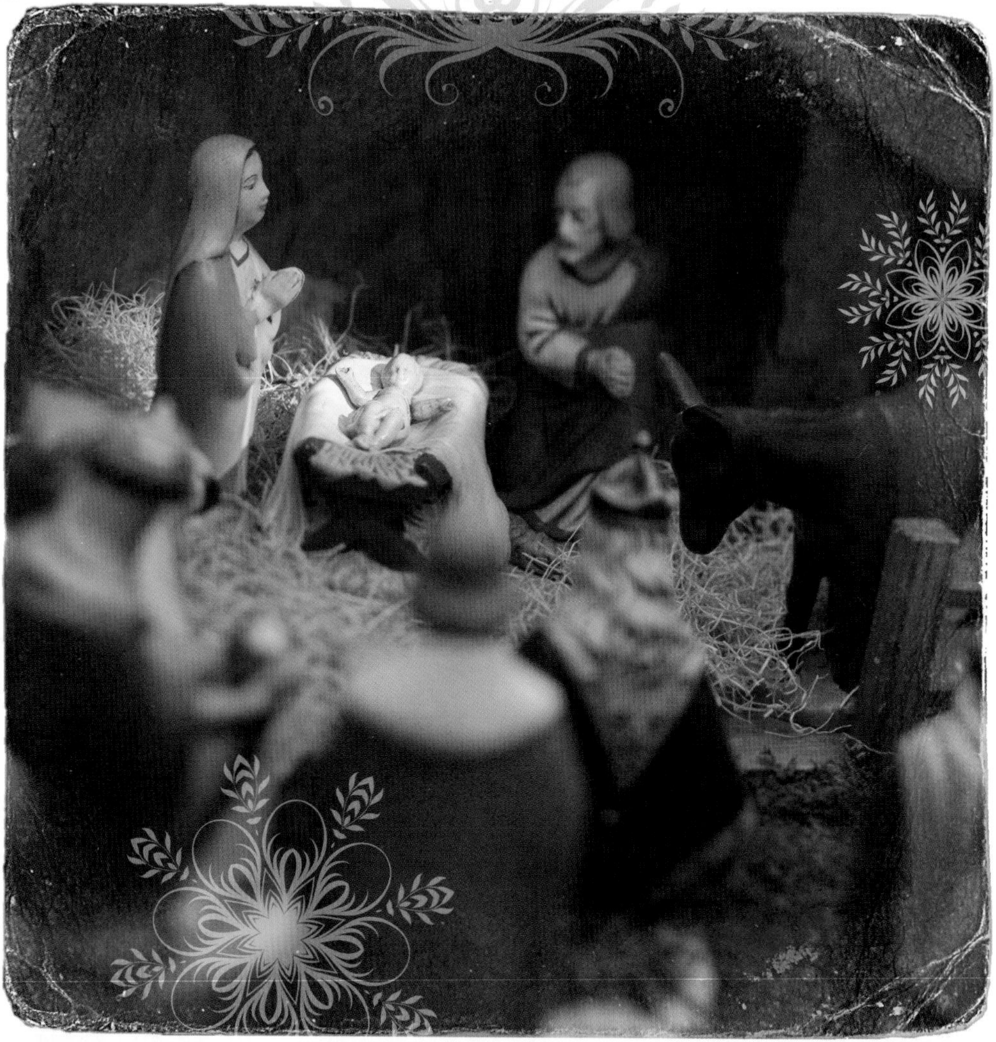

❧

"*Danke*," said the old woman, with a smile. She took Dad's coat and Mom's and laid them on the sofa, and that's when she spied me.

I cannot describe the look that came into her eyes as she studied my face. "Oh, Ollie," she said, hobbling near me. Her hand revealed a slight tremor as it reached out and caressed my hair. "Oh, my Ollie, it has been so long. Look at you! Look how you've grown."

Her eyes filled with tears as she pulled me into an embrace. She quivered with emotion, but when she released me, her face was glowing. "Oh, Ollie," she said, "I thought I vould never see you again. Come over to your *Oma*. And look at you, so happy and so strong and so big! You so remind me of your *Opa*."

Her wiry arms encircled me again, and I felt her kissing the top of my head. I started to pull away, but I didn't. After one more, "My Ollie," she turned abruptly and headed to the kitchen.

"*Aber was den! All is ready,*" she said. "Elke, help me set the table." My mom obligingly found some dishes in the cabinet, while Frau Reinhart pulled silverware from a drawer. Then out came the ham and the beans and carrots, along with a German potato salad and some sauerkraut. The meal wasn't as my mom would have prepared it. It was sort of vinegary and mustardy, but it was good, and I ate every bite—except the kraut.

All the while, Frau Reinhart was talking, half in German, half in English, about family matters that didn't make any sense at all to me. Each of us tried to contribute to the conversation, but it seemed lost on the old woman. Her hearing was gone, and her mind nearly so. But her heart was warm, and she kept the conversation flowing all by herself. She spoke of long ago days, recalling happier times with Dietrich—her husband, I gathered—and with her son Gunther, who had apparently been a bookkeeper, and about his wife, Elke. Occasionally she said something that seemed funny to her, and she laughed and laughed, and we laughed along with her.

All the while she kept stealing glances in my direction, and whenever she did her eyes sparkled. A couple of times I winked at her, and she seemed as delighted as a girl caught under the mistletoe.

After the cake and coffee—the eggnog never showed up—we relocated to the parlor where Mrs. Reinhart went right to the tree and started handing out gifts. There was a simple necklace for my mom, a tie and socks for my dad, and a pair of new shoes for me. It was all great fun. Then my mother handed the last remaining package to the old woman. Frau Reinhart opened the present and clutched the red sweater to herself with motions of delight.

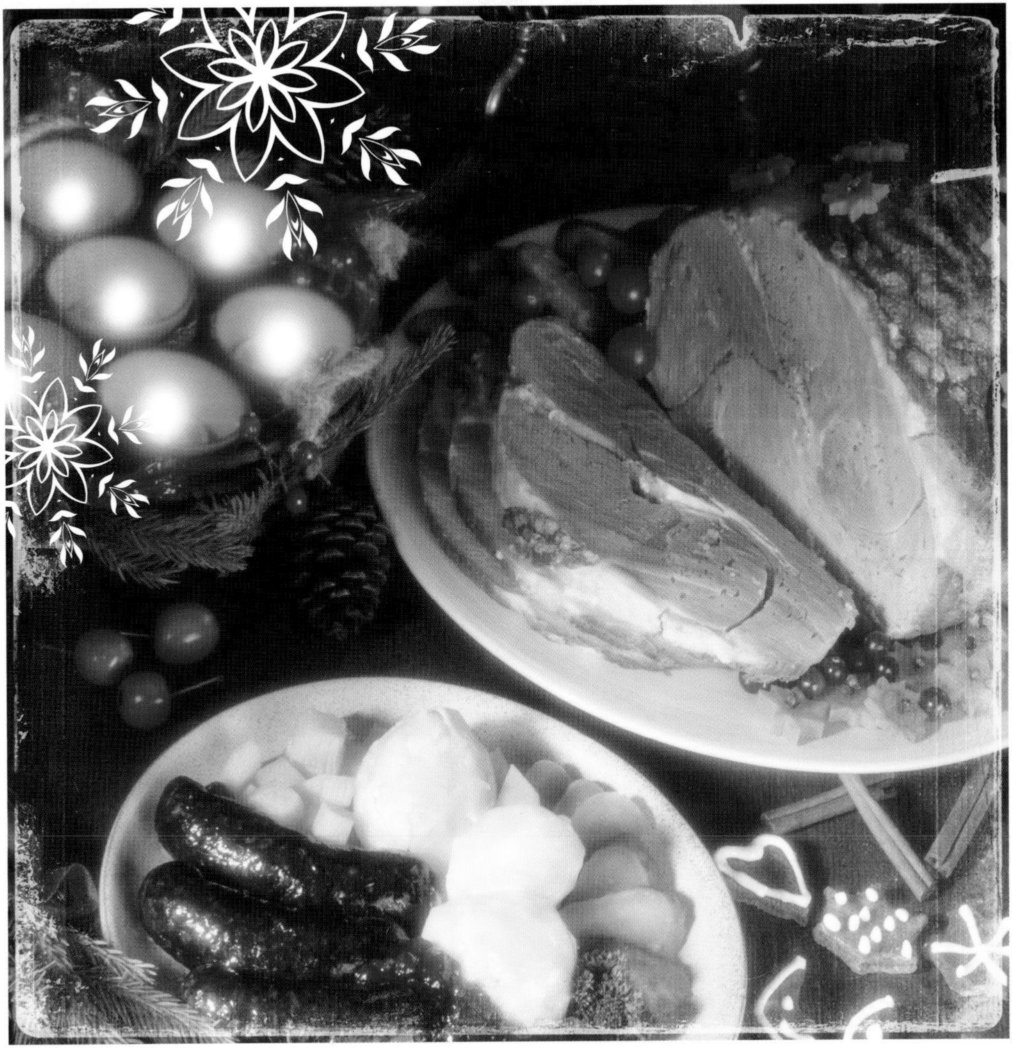

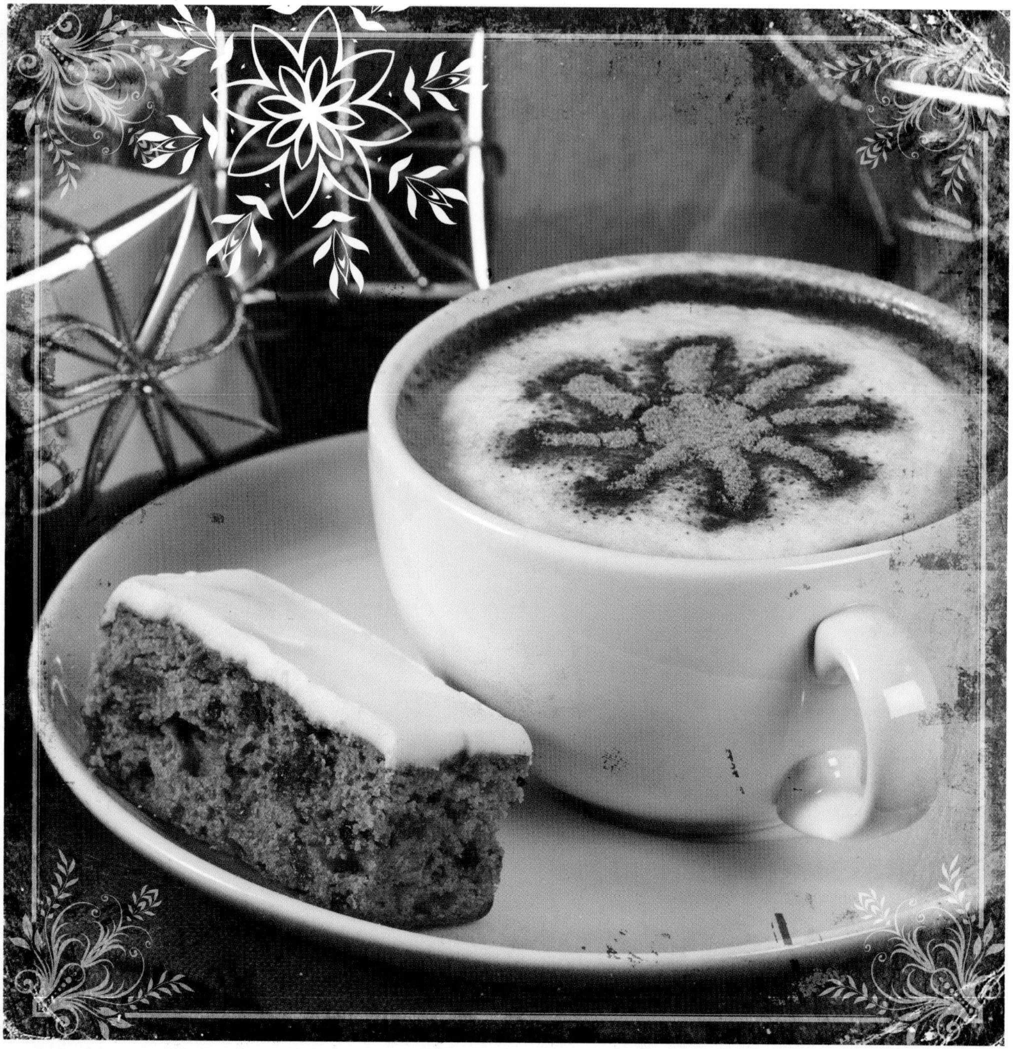

"*Oh, danke, danke*! It is *wunderbar*," she said. "But the most vonderful thing is to have you all here with me." Then she lowered her voice almost to a whisper and said, "One night, in that awful place, I was so frightened, especially for Ollie. I had forgotten what time of year it vas, all vas so dark and so dreadful. Everyone vas so sick. And then from somewhere down the hall, I heard another prisoner singing, 'Silent night, holy night, all is calm, all is bright . . .' And I recalled that it was Christmas. And that night in the jail, I remembered a little poem we used to say on Christmas Eve:

Silent, holy, calm, and bright,
Jesus came to pierce the night.
Jesus came to make things right.
So be . . .
Silent, holy, calm, and bright,
. . . tonight.

"And that's when I knew that everything vould be all right, someday, somehow, someway, some place. Perhaps not now, but then; perhaps not here, but there."

She was quiet for a moment. But the next thing I knew, she was on her feet again and headed to the fireplace. She picked up the snow globe from the mantle and shook it in our direction, saying, "Except for the clothes on my back, this is the only I thing I brought with me out of *Deutschland*."

She wound up the music, and it played "Silent Night." We listened and it seemed like music from far away and long ago. No one said anything for a long time. Then the old woman, suddenly looking very tired, said, "Vell, it is time for bed. Oh, it vould have broken my heart had you not come. But here you are! And my Ollie has come to wish his *Oma* a *Frohe Weihnachten*. God bless you for it, my grandson."

I nodded as best I could. We rose, put on our coats, and moved toward the door.

"Vait!" called the old woman. She picked up the globe and brought it to me. "You must have this, Ollie," she said. "It's the only thing I can give you from *Deutschland*, and you must take it so you'll always remember that God looked into our globe and saw our grief. We look in His manger and see His answer."

Well, I looked at Dad, he looked at Mom, and she looked at me. I took the globe from the woman's hands, sat it on the floor, and gave her the

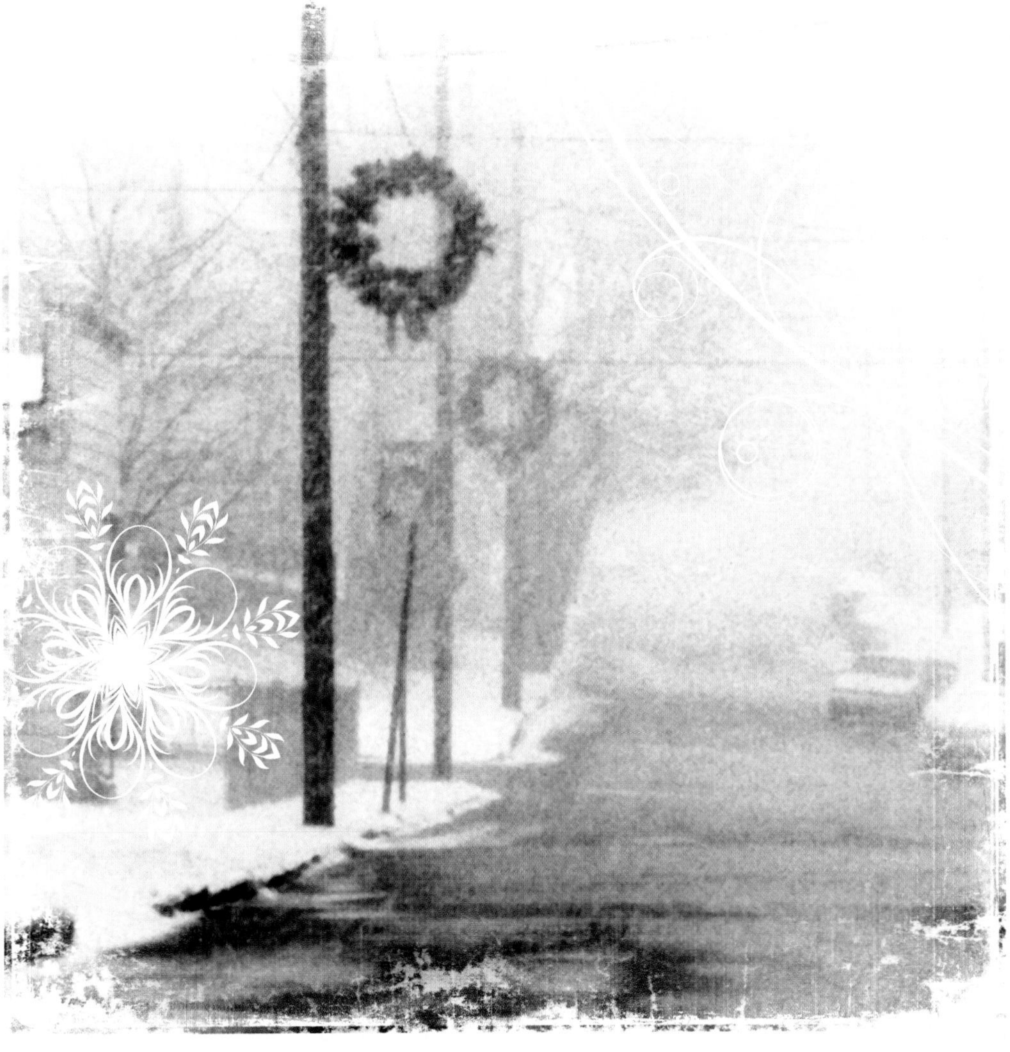

hardest hug I'd given anyone in my life. Then I picked it up carefully and ducked out the door because no one wants to see a twelve-year-old boy get the sniffles.

I heard my parents exiting behind me, saying things like, "*Gute Nacht*," and "*Auf Wiedersehen*," and after exchanging cars in the carport, we drove home in silence.

We visited Frau Reinhart several times afterward, but she didn't seem to know us. The spell was broken, and her mind was gone. Shortly afterward, a small item appeared in the local paper:

> *Frau Alfreda Reinhart, 88, formerly of Munich, died at her residence on Elm Street yesterday with her parish priest in attendance. She was preceded in death by a husband, a sister, a son, a daughter-in-law, and a grandson.*

❋ ❋ ❋

Well, that's the story as my dad told it to me. But he wasn't quite finished. He went on to say, "And that's why, son, every year since I was your age, I've picked up this old globe on Christmas Eve, turned it over, wound it up, and listened to its music. And as I see the snow swirling around the manger, I think of the night my folks and I were able to give an old woman her family back for one last Christmas Eve. And I remember her poem and her words, for they are true. The good Lord looked into our globe and saw our grief. We look into His manger and see His answer. And that's why Christmas is silent and holy and calm and bright."

For a long time we sat there in front of the dying fire, saying nothing. I might have gotten the sniffles if my dad hadn't told me that no one wanted to see a twelve-year-old boy do that. So I finally got up, yawned real big, and headed to bed. After all, I didn't want to oversleep on Christmas morning.

"Good night, Dad," I said as I headed toward the bedroom. I turned back and saw him gazing again at that glass ball filled with water and wonder. "Good night, Dad," I said again. "Sleep well."

He smiled and waved me on to bed. "Good night, Ollie," he said. "You sleep well too."

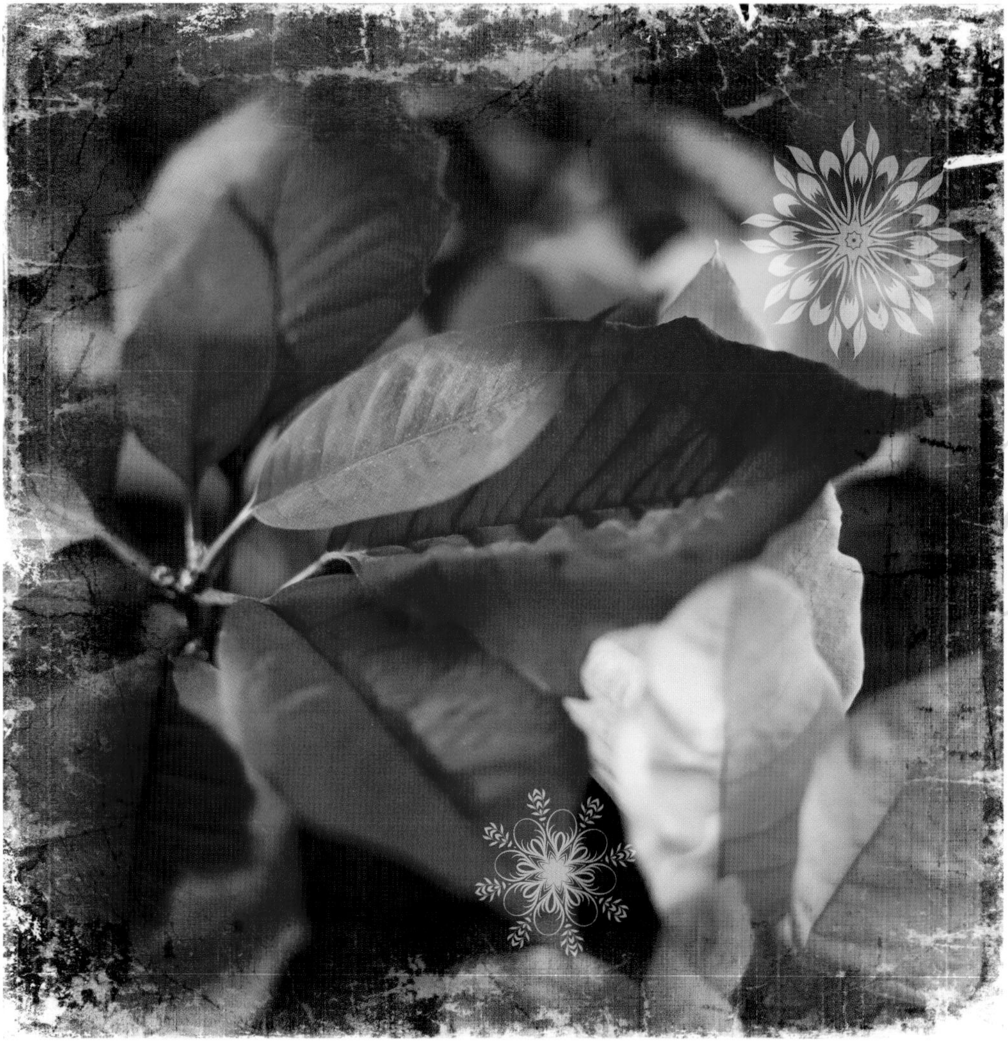

Poet Boy

obert Louis Brendleton lived at the end of a quaint lane just outside Hockley-by-the-Sea, on the outskirts of New Haven. Though neither of his parents was actually British, they listened to the BBC every morning, served hot tea most afternoons at four, and the supper menu on any given night might include Yorkshire pudding, cottage pie, or asparagus mimosa.

Robert Louis' father, Dr. Albert Brendleton, was professor of Shakespeare and Renaissance Literature at St. Andrew's University, where he lectured with a perceptible British accent. Robbie's mother, Dr. Elizabeth Brendleton, taught Victorian poetry at the same institution. Robert Louis was their only child, and he was known for his photographic memory and high grades, though he was a retiring boy and suffered terribly from shyness, timidity, and stage fright. He was happiest when secluded in the reading nook of the library adjacent to his bedroom. There he perused many a quaint and curious volume of forgotten lore.

One Saturday in early October, Robert Louis was in the reading nook, nearly napping, when he heard the Westminster chimes of the doorbell. There were noises of footsteps and door openings and greetings, and Robert Louis heard a familiar voice floating through the house like a piccolo: "Robbie Louie, Robbie Louie, are you here? Come, come. I have exciting news!"

Aunt Clotilda could hardly wait. "Robbie Louie," she said as he entered the room, "I have written a stage play, and I need a well-versed, fourteen-year-old boy as the narrator and chief actor. Do you know such a boy?"

Robert Louis stood speechless, but he shook his head vigorously.

"Well, we have such a boy in this very room, Robbie Louie, for I have chosen you to play the immortal role of the carpenter Joseph, betrothed husband to the virginal Mary."

Robbie tried to reply, but couldn't.

"It's for the Christmas Eve service in the university chapel," she said. "The committee asked me to write an original production, and I have entitled it: 'By the Shores of Eternity' by Dr. Clotilda Brendleton. The part of Joseph is written just for you. And you will be pleased to know that Ruby Ascot has already consented to play the role of Mary."

"Oh, oh . . . Aunt Clotilda . . ." —but nothing more came from Robert Louis' mouth.

"I have worked on this stage play for months," continued Aunt Clotilda. "It has been a long-cherished dream of mine. We will tell the

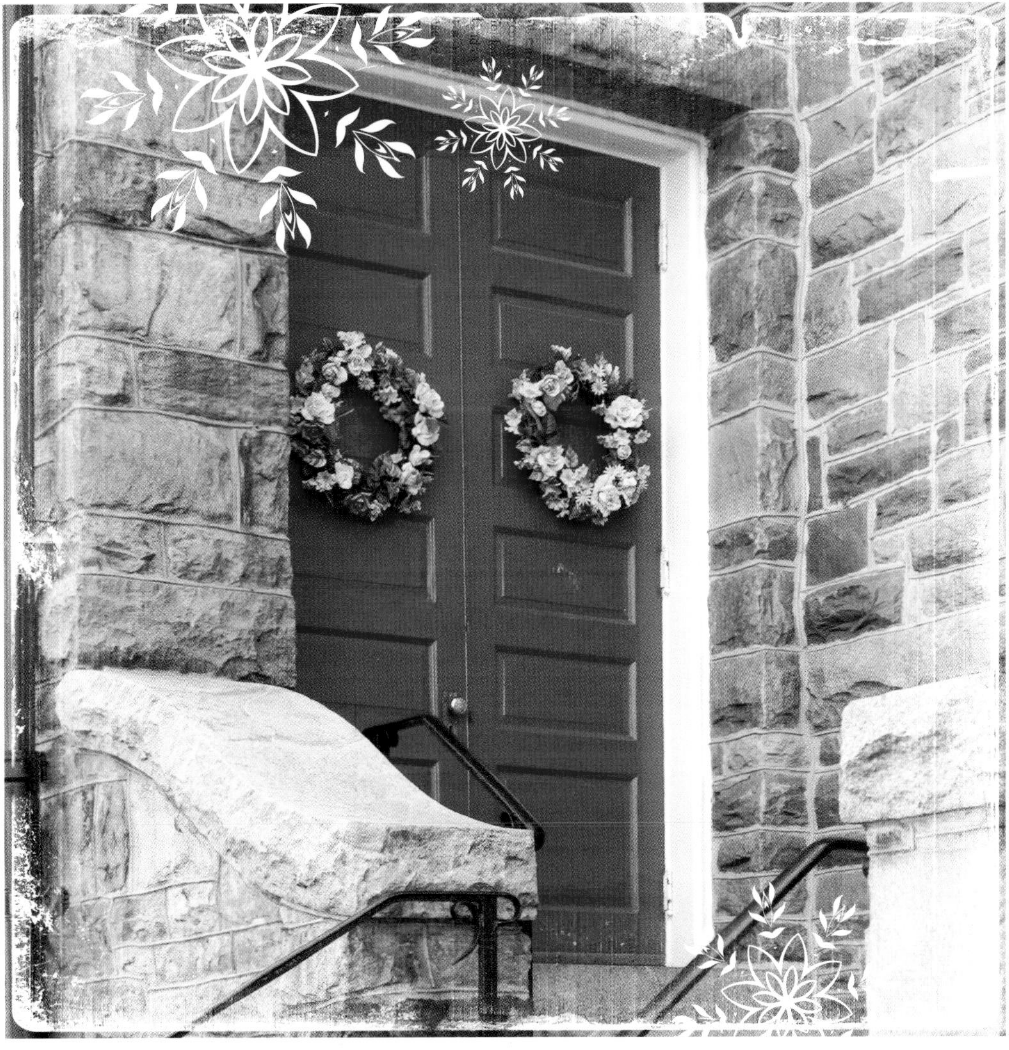

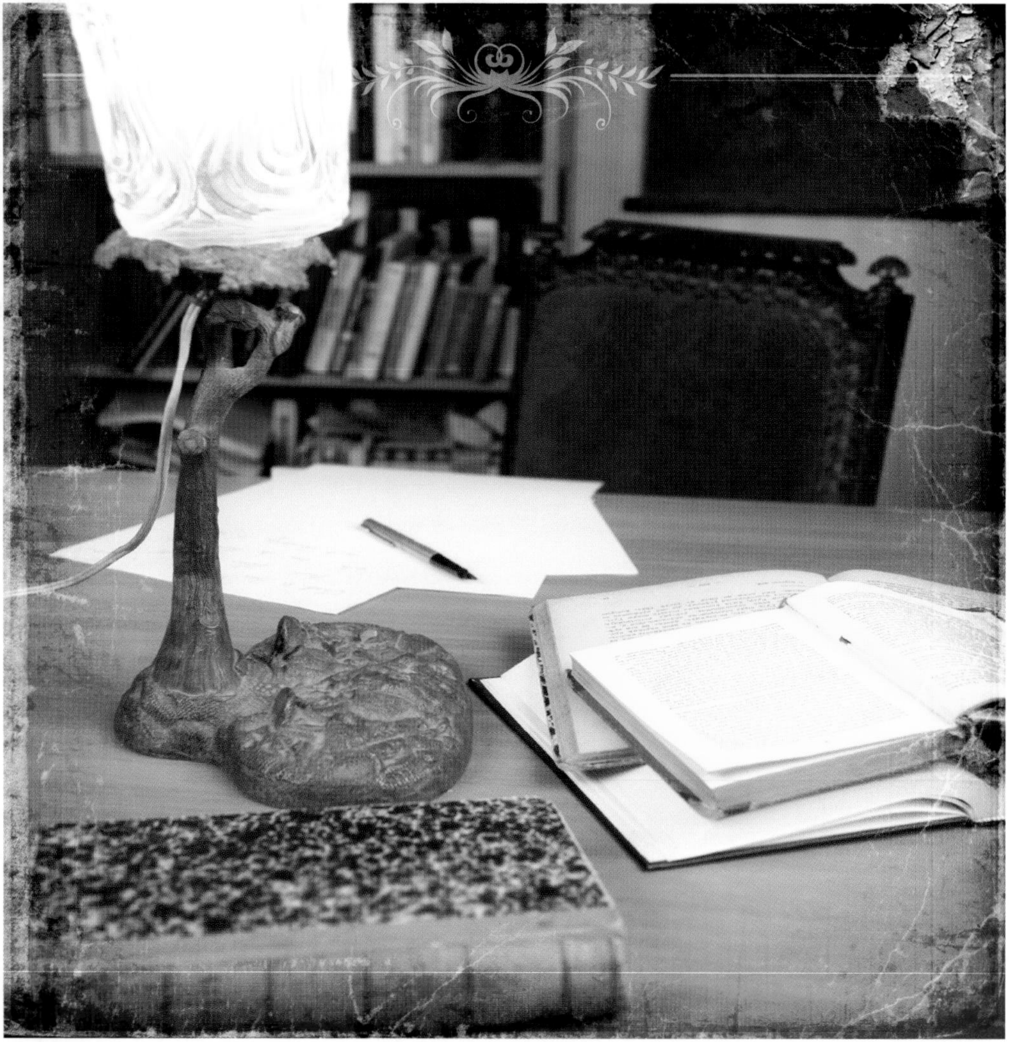

Christmas story, and your opening lines will be: 'By the shores, by the shores of eternity, where time has intersected infinity, a baby was born one night.' Here's the script. I am sure that with your gifts, you'll have it memorized in no time."

"Oh, oh . . . Aunt Clotilda . . ."

And that's how Robert Louis Brendleton found himself standing backstage on December 24th, sweating through his costume, peeking at the packed house with its encircling gallery, and wishing he were dead.

But he did *not* die, and at precisely seven o'clock, the curtain rose. Robbie was encircled by a spot of light that seemed brighter than the sun. He was too blinded to see the audience and too frightened to speak. He thought of turning and running, but his feet were glued to the floor. His mind was as blank as if someone had swiped it with an eraser. He tried mightily to remember those opening lines—"By the shores, by the shores of eternity, where time has intersected infinity, a baby was born one night."

But all that came out of his mouth was: "Oh, oh . . ."

After several anxious moments, he heard Aunt Clotilda whispering through the back curtain: "By the shores . . . by the shores . . ."

A single drop of oxygen entered Robbie's lungs. He closed his eyes and blurted out the first words that came to mind:

By the shores of Gitche Gumee,
By the shining Big-Sea-Water,
Stood the wigwam of Nokomis,
Daughter of the Moon, Nokomis.
Dark behind it rose the forest,
Rose the black and gloomy pine-trees,
Rose the firs with cones upon them;
Bright before it beat the water,
Beat the clear and sunny water,
Beat the shining Big-Sea-Water.

He stopped abruptly, and the house was as quiet as the air after an explosion. Then Robert Louis meekly cleared his throat and said, "Henry Wadsworth Longfellow, 1807 to 1882."

There was a muttering of noise from the audience and a sparse bit of applause, followed by additional moments of awkward silence. Then with a mighty shove, Aunt Clotilda sent Ruby Ascot spinning onto the stage.

Ruby was dressed in a pale robe and looked as though she were about to give birth to a large pillow. She seemed frightened, though one

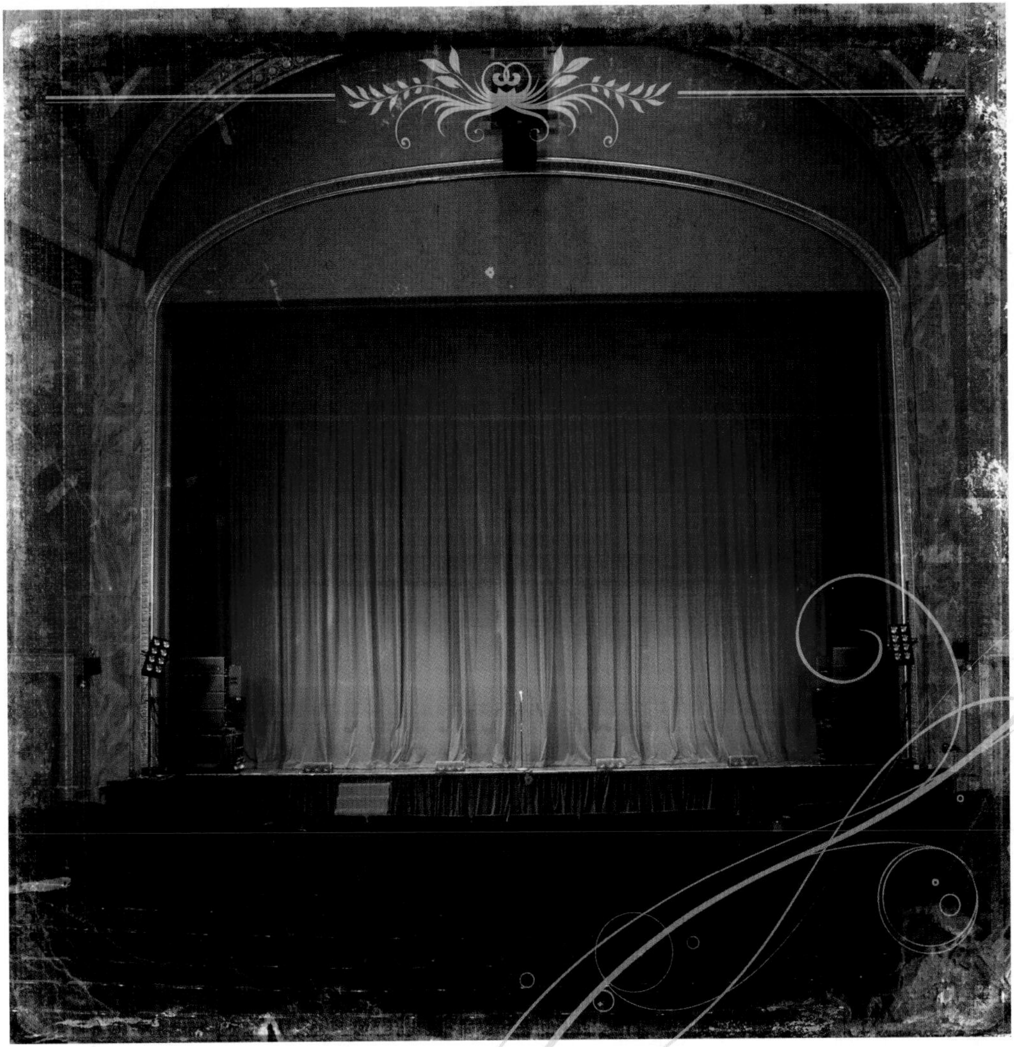

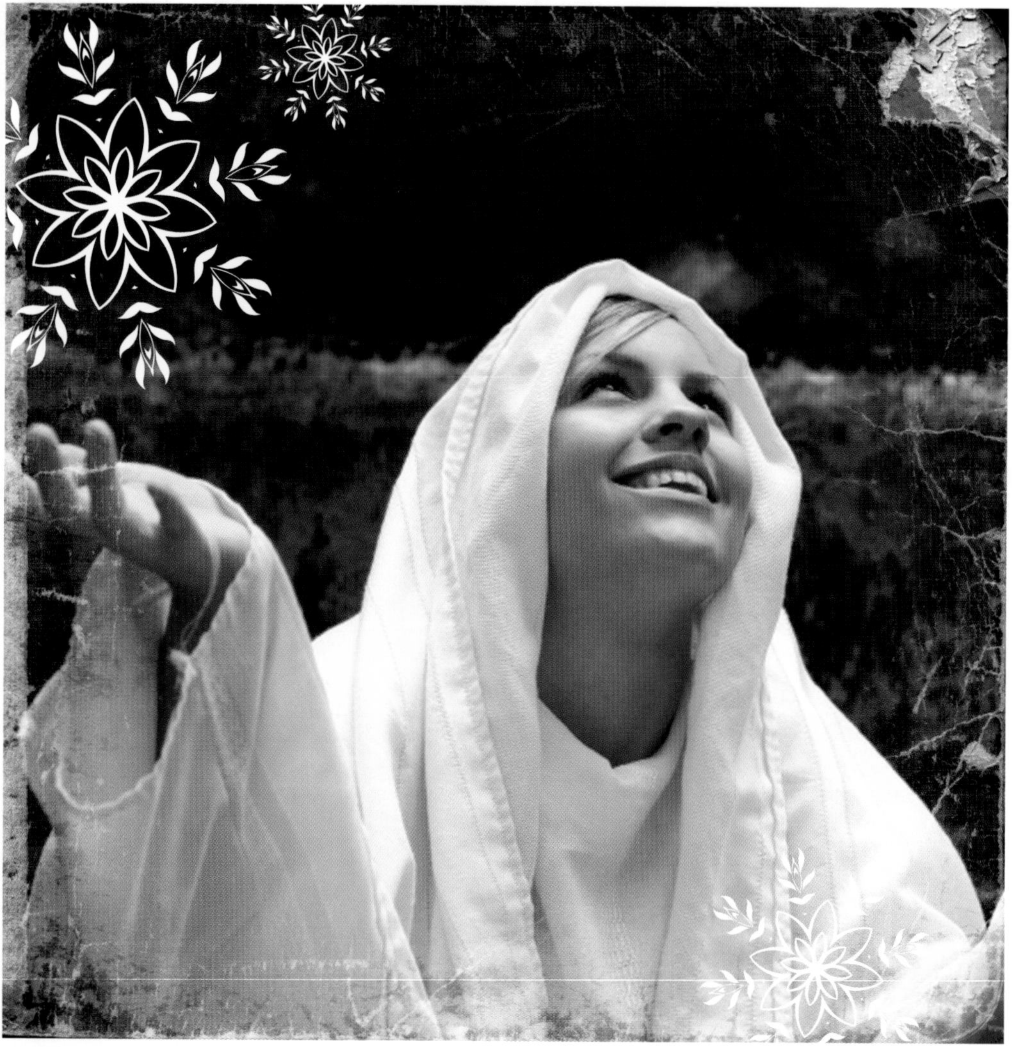

couldn't tell whether it was real or put-on. But in either case, she had no problem remembering the magnificent lines Aunt Clotilda had written for her. "Joseph!" she cried dramatically. "Oh, Joseph, how much farther to Bethlehem? The day is far passed, the night is on the wing, and I am great with child. My mind is perplexed with many an imponderable and unanswerable question, and my heart is sore troubled. What says your heart, oh, Joseph?"

Robbie said nothing, so at length Ruby repeated her last line, and then she repeated it twice more. "What says your heart, oh Joseph? What says your heart?"

Robbie looked into space and replied:

My heart's in the Highlands,
my heart is not here,

My hearts in the Highlands,
a-chasing the deer;
Chasing the wild deer, and
following the roe,
My heart's in the Highlands, wherever I go.

Ruby stared at Robbie with bewilderment, but all he said was, "Robert Burns, 1759 to 1796."

It seemed at that moment the entire production might collapse, but from behind the curtain came Aunt Clotilda's strident voice with the next lines: "Listen . . . listen, listen . . ." A flash of recognition came into Robbie's eyes, and he said: "Listen, my children, and you shall hear . . ."

But Ruby cut him off. "Listen, Joseph," she said. "Listen to my questions and reassure my heart. How came we to this point? Whence our divine direction? How came you to lead me down this weary road of Jewish suffering and hope?"

"I shall be telling this with a sigh," replied Robbie after a long pause.

I shall be telling this with a sigh
Somewhere ages and ages hence:
Two roads diverged in a wood, and I—
I took the one less traveled by,
And that has made all the difference.

Robbie was just about to say the words, "Robert Frost," when Ruby fumbled for her next line. "And what a difference. All the difference. Yes, and a good difference it is. But, Joseph," she said, recovering, "can we make it onward? I know we can. Look yonder, far ahead of us. Are those the hills of Judea? Are those the mountains of David?"

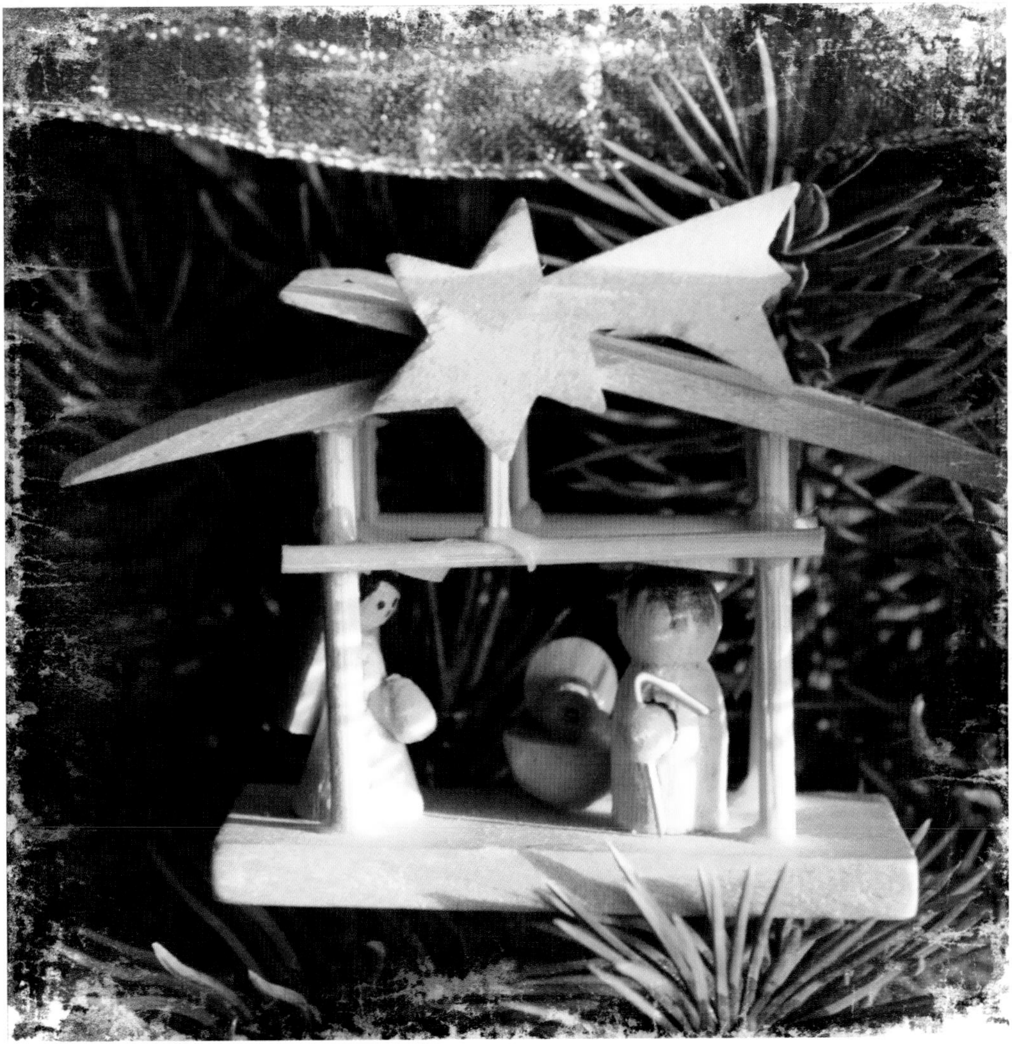

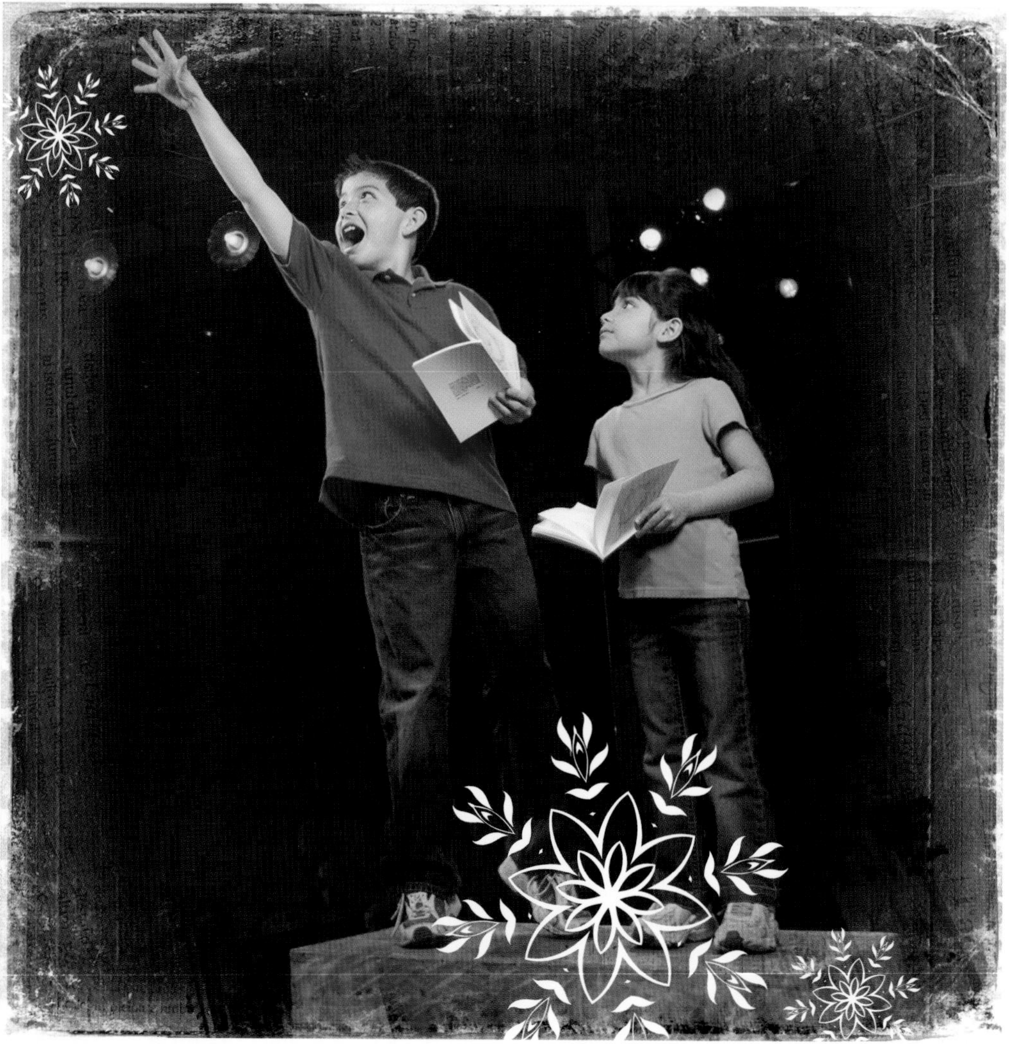

Robbie looked into the spotlight as if trying to see the mountains of David.

"The mountains they are silent folk," he said at last.

They stand afar—alone,
And the clouds that kiss their bows at night
Hear neither sigh nor groan.
Each bears him in his ordered place
As soldiers do, and bold and high
They fold their forests round their feet
And bolster up the sky.

Just as Robbie was about to credit those words to the American poet Hamlin Garland, Ruby spoke up. "Well, let's go onward," she said with confusion, "onward toward the hills. I can go if you will go, and we can go if I will go, and we shall go if He will help us, and He *will* go . . . and we shall make a go of it."

"Yes," said Joseph with a gulp, "the woods are lovely, dark, and deep, but I have promises to keep, and miles to go before I sleep."

And with that the curtain fell on Act 1.

Since no one could figure out how to keep the curtain from rising for Act 2, the players got into position. The scene was the outskirts of Bethlehem, and this time Mary opened with a long soliloquy, which gave Robbie a bit of time to recover his nerves. He actually listened to her as she recalled the angelic visitor that told her she would bear the Son of God. Ruby ended her speech by nobly saying, "My soul glorifies the Lord and my spirit rejoices in God my Savior, for he has been mindful of the humble state of his servant. From now on all generations will call me blessed" (Luke 1:46–48 NIV).

She looked expectantly at Joseph, whose lines called for tender affirmation. "Oh, Mary," he said, "how do I love thee? Let me count the ways. I love thee to the depth and breadth and height my soul can reach, when feeling out of sight . . . I love thee to the level of every day's most quiet need, by sun and candlelight."

Somehow the words didn't seem quite right, but they didn't seem quite wrong. So the weary couple turned and entered the little cardboard town of Bethlehem.

The play continued through Act 2 with Joseph uttering not a single word that had actually been written for him. Instead the most unexpected snatches of poetry came from his mouth, and somehow they increasingly seemed to fit, if just barely. But the time the Christ child arrived, Robbie had found that his breathing was more normal. It was his memory that was working strangely. It invariably bypassed Aunt Clotilda's lines, seizing

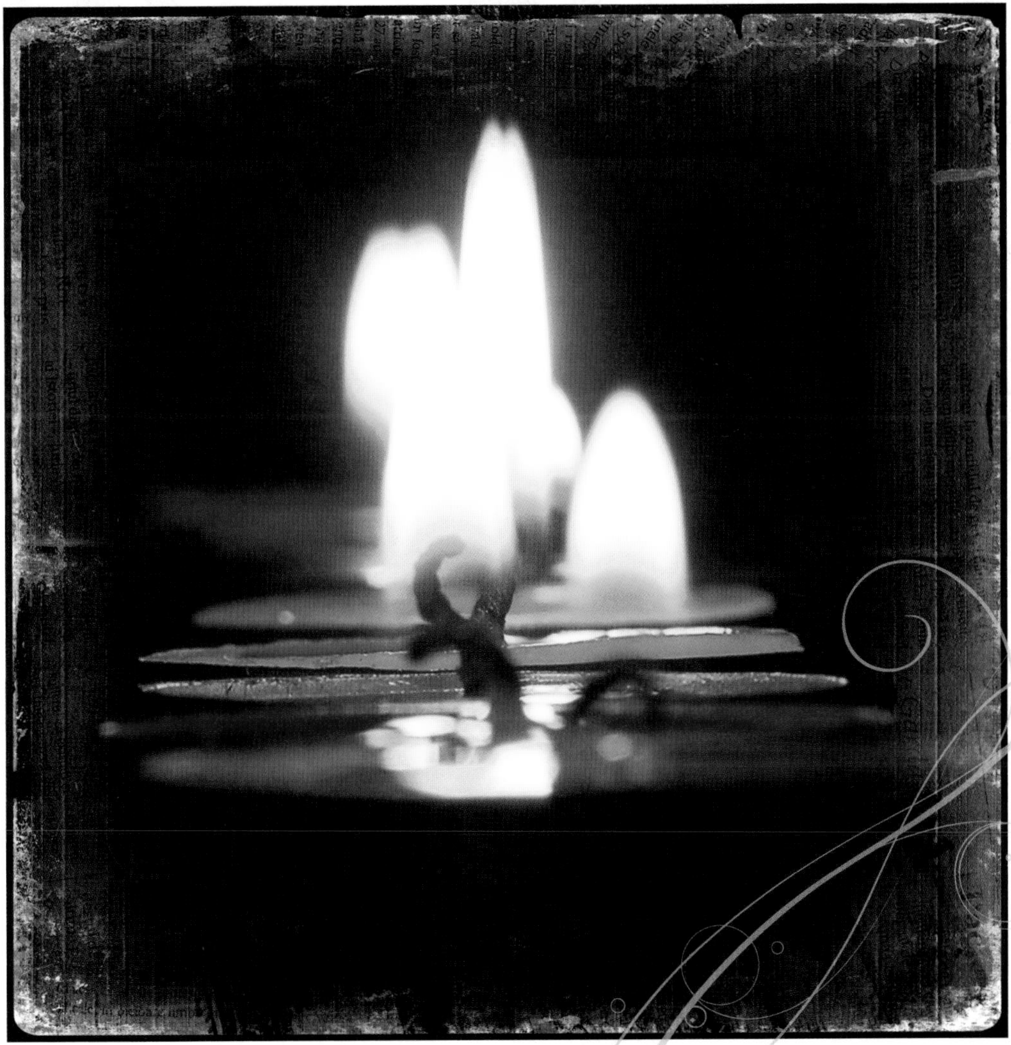

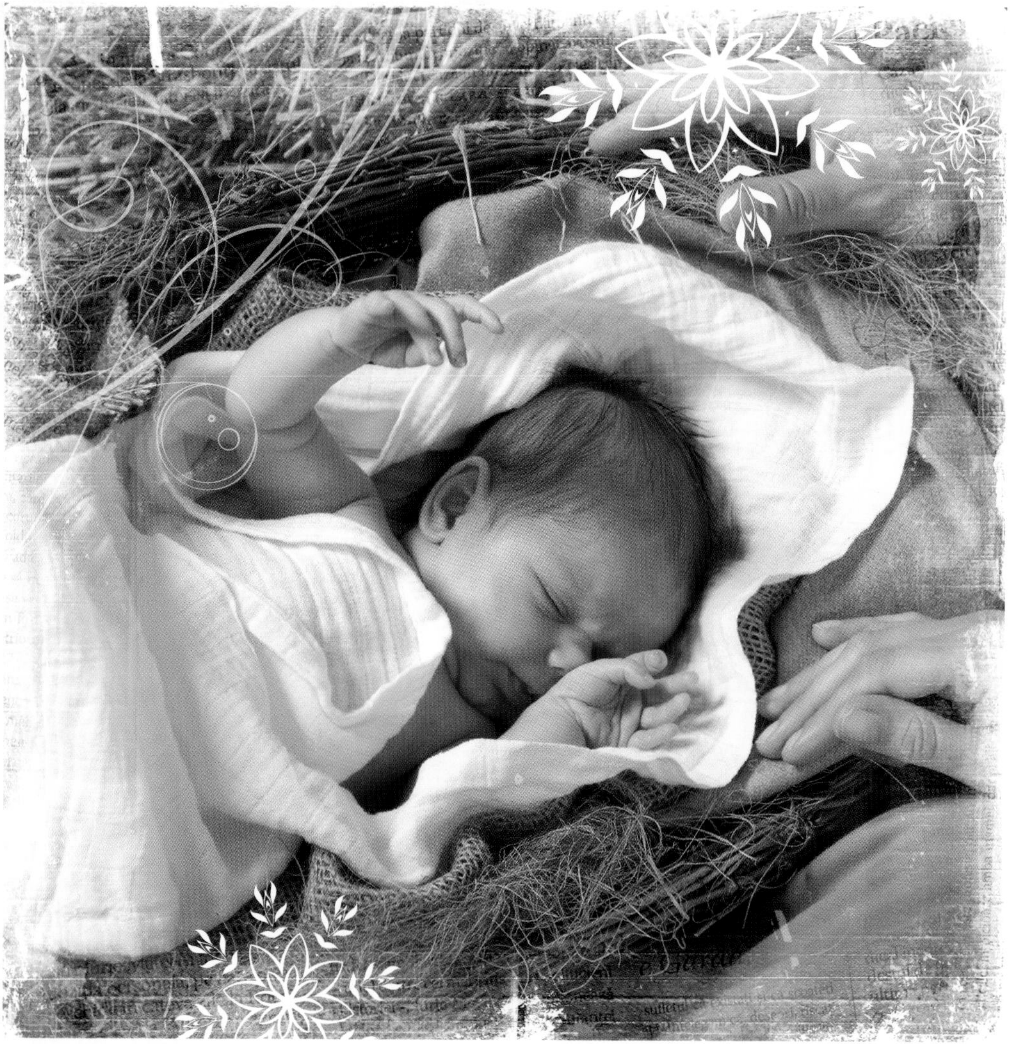

instead on various poems and stanzas and verses long ago tucked away in the photographic files of his internal library.

Some audience members actually wiped away a tear when Robbie quoted the simple lines from the Detroit writer, Edgar A. Guest:

Let's be brave when the trials come

And our hearts are sad and
our lips are dumb,

Let's strengthen ourselves
in the times of test

By whispering softly
that God knows best;

Let us still believe, though we
cannot know,

We shall learn sometime it is better so.

And so it was in the final act that as Joseph stood looking down at the Babe in the manger, there was absolute silence in the church as he recited the ancient words of St. Germanus from the eighth century:

A great and mighty wonder,
A full and holy cure!
The Virgin bears the Infant
With virgin honor pure.
The Word becomes Incarnate,
And yet remains on high,
And Cherubim sing anthems
To shepherds from the sky.
And we with them triumphant
Repeat the hymn again:
"To God on high be glory,
And peace on earth to men."

At last the angels departed, the shepherds returned to their fields, the Babe was carried offstage in the tender arms of the virginal Mary, and Joseph was left in the spotlight for his final lines. No one doubts that Aunt Clotilda had prepared a wonderful closing monologue, but no one heard it that night. Robbie found other words tucked away in the vaults of his memory. They were 1500 years old, but they seemed as fresh as the youngest child.

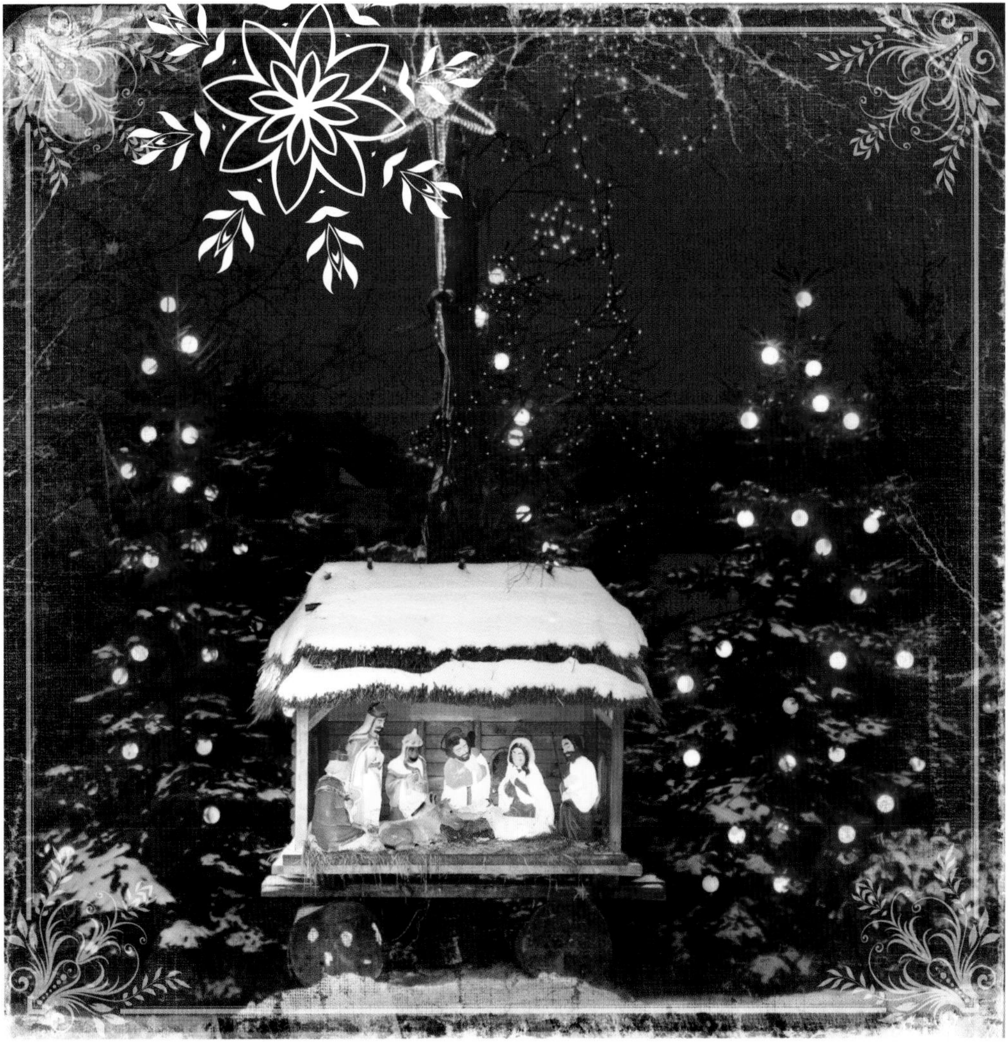

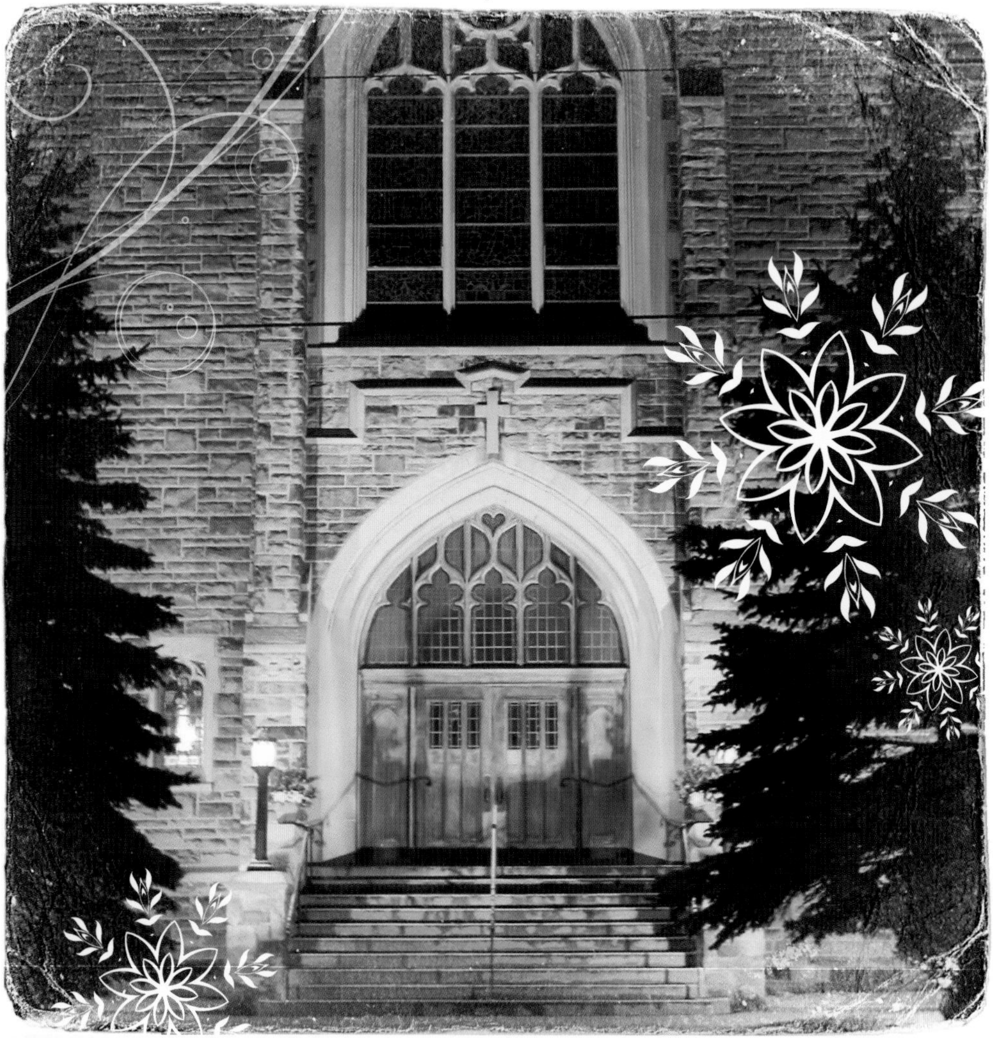

Of the Father's love begotten, ere the worlds began to be,
He is Alpha and Omega, He the source, the ending He,
Of the things that are, that have been,
And that future years shall see—evermore and evermore!

O that birth forever blessèd, when the virgin, full of grace,
By the Holy Ghost conceiving, bare the Savior of our race;
And the Babe, the world's Redeemer,
First revealed His sacred face—evermore and evermore!

O ye heights of heaven adore Him; angel hosts, His praises sing;
Powers, dominions, bow before Him, and extol our God and King!
Let no tongue on earth be silent,
Every voice in concert sing, evermore and evermore!

Christ, to Thee with God the Father, and, O Holy Ghost, to Thee,
Hymn and chant with high thanksgiving, and unwearied praises be:
Honor, glory, and dominion,
And eternal victory, evermore and evermore!

The church was absolutely silent. The audience was enthralled by the story of the Christ child, and no one was ready to break the spell—and so Robert Louis did it for them. For the first time that evening, he smiled; and as he smiled he said:

> *But I heard him exclaim, ere he drove out of sight,*
> *"Happy Christmas to all, and to all a good-night!"*

❄ ❄ ❄

It took a full month for Robert Louis Brendleton to recover his nerves—and a good deal longer for Aunt Clotilda to do the same. But in the town of Hockley-by-the-Sea, the university community of St. Andrews is still talking about the night when the poet boy uttered words from the secret channels of his memory to show us afresh that . . .

. . . by the shores of eternity, where time intersects infinity, a baby was born one night.

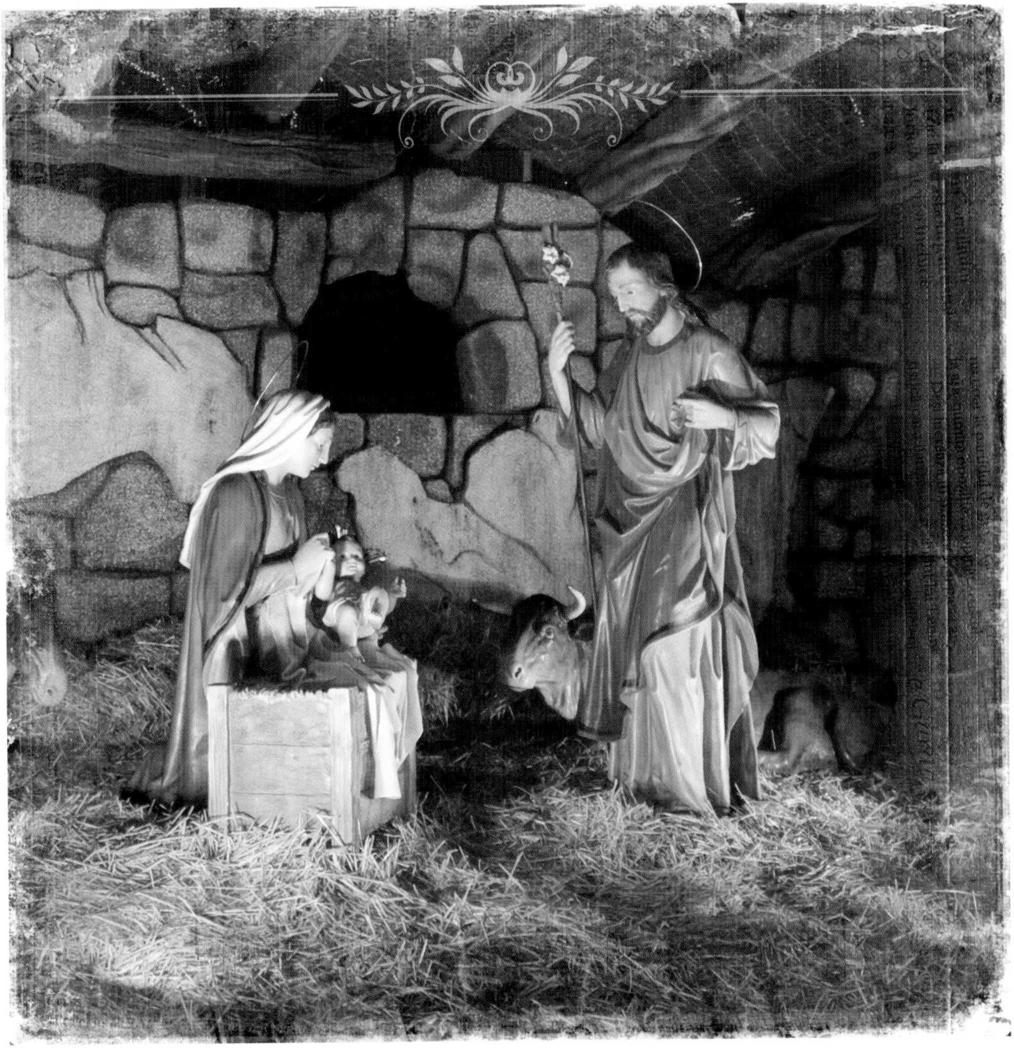

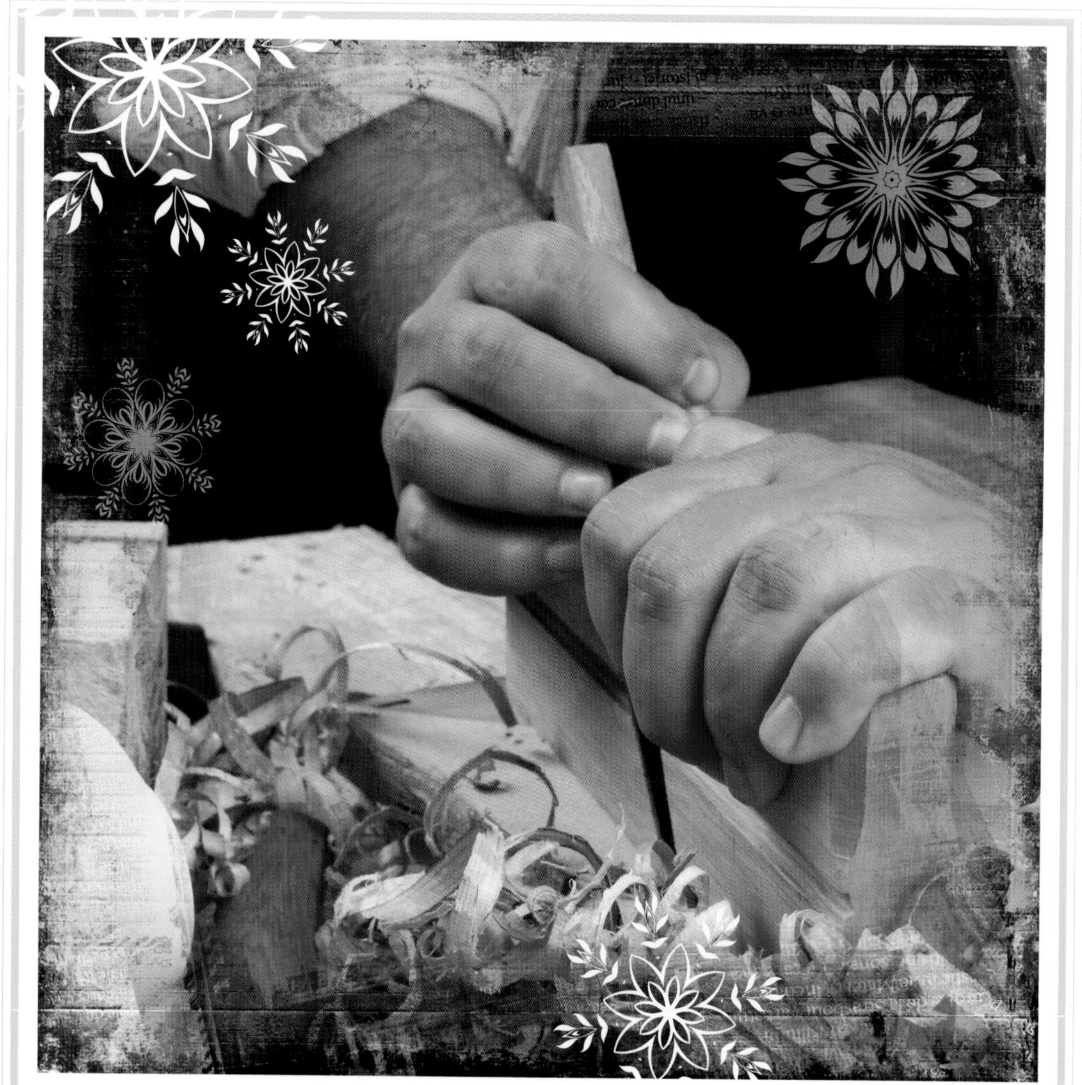

Over My Dead Body

h," said Max Schroeder, his wrinkled face softening and forming a smile, "and have it you shall—over my dead body."

Young Kasper didn't know what to make of his grandfather's well-rehearsed, oft-repeated answer. Nor did anyone else. It was a reply designed to prick the mind while shutting the mouth. And it was spoken indiscriminately, to one and all, to the grandson on his lap, to the curator in the museum, to the pope in the Vatican. For everyone on earth, it seemed, wanted to buy, steal, inherit, or otherwise acquire Max Schroeder's most famous work of all—his thumb-in-mouth nativity.

But the old woodcarver would only offer it "over my dead body"—terms which his daughter Johanna didn't like at all. "Why," she once exclaimed, "he's practically inviting a thief to murder him for it."

※ ※ ※

Max had whittled out his career by accident, for as a boy he had needed something to occupy his time while watching his Uncle Karl's sheep in the hills above Lake Lucerne during warm summer months. One day out of boredom—there are no wolves in the Alps—he had extracted his Swiss army knife from the pocket of his knickers and started carving a sheep's face onto the crook of his staff. By age twelve, Max, no fool, was making more money in a week by selling his wooden sheep in Lucerne than he could make in a month by tending his uncle's real ones.

By age fifteen, he was supporting himself nicely. By his twenties, his artistry was sought throughout central Europe, and by his thirties, Max was set for life. One original hand-carved Schroeder Sheep, sold in his own studio in Lucerne, would fetch a very high price indeed.

They were, after all, remarkably winsome sheep. Some were thick with wool, while others seemed lately sheered. Some were old and fat. Others were young and frisky. Most stood on all fours and seemed quite sheepish. But a whimsical few—those in Schroeder's Singular Sheep Collection—stood on hind legs, reading books through wire-rimmed spectacles, playing instruments or cards, spinning hoops, directing traffic, or even giving lectures.

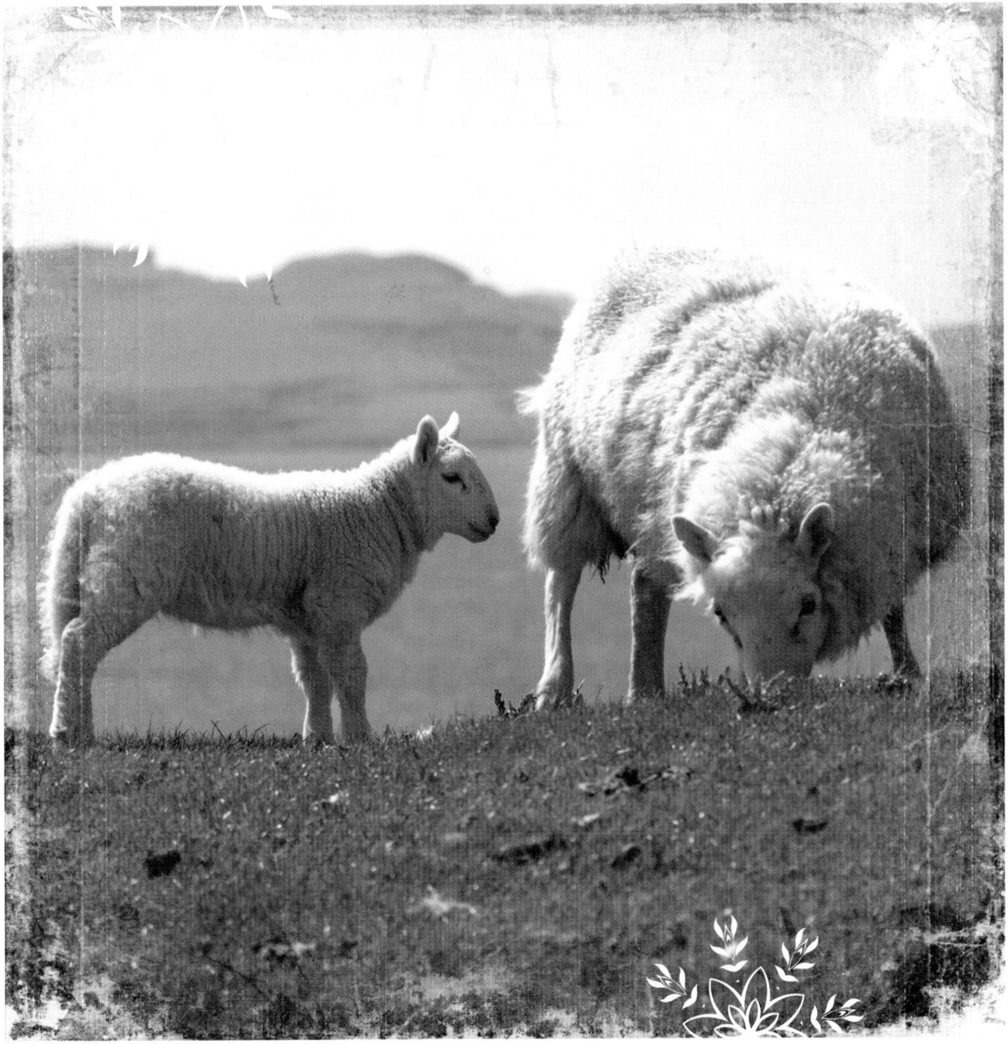

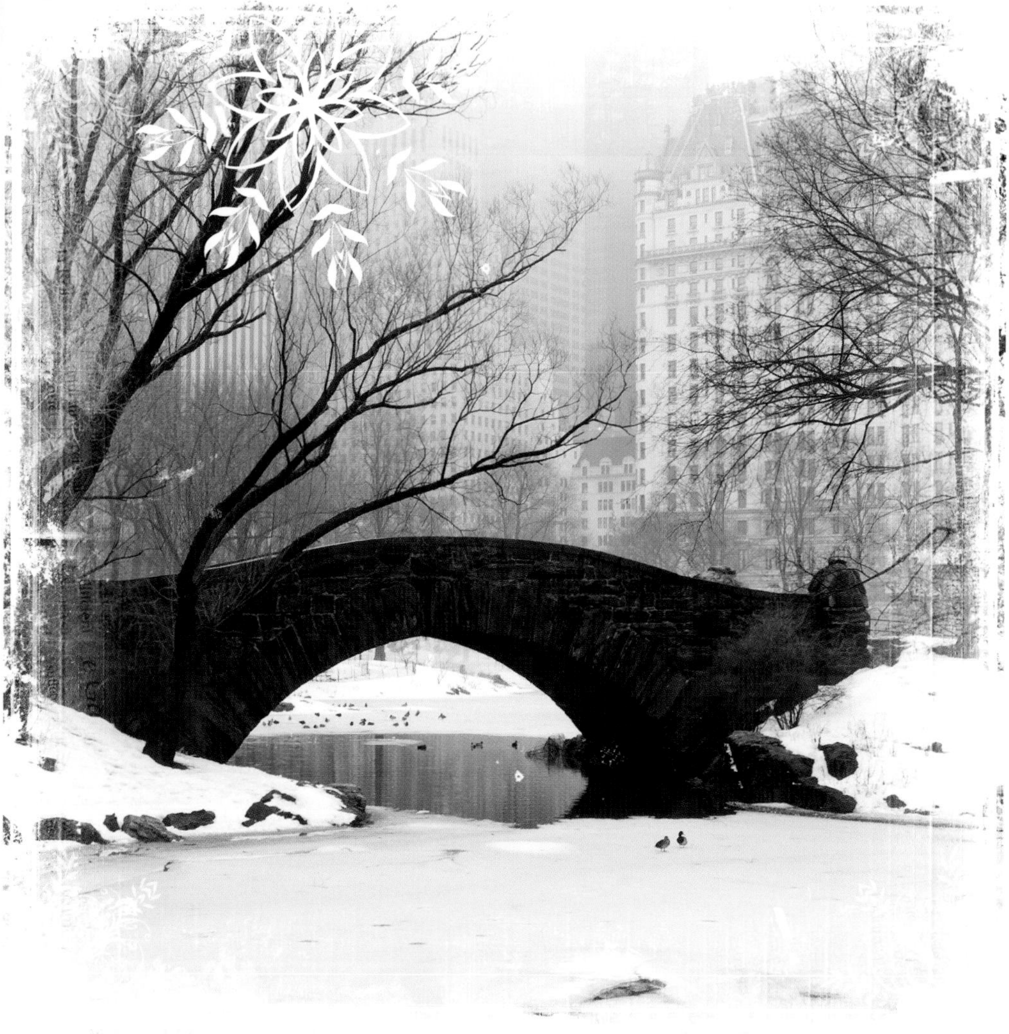

When the French magazine *Le Monde* ran a feature article on "The Shepherd of a Thousand Wooden Sheep," demand for his works doubled, and the price tags on his wooden animals tripled. Every penny went into a numbered Swiss account in Zurich, which Max tended with the diligence of the biblical shepherd who nightly numbered his flock. You might say he was fleecing his public most effectively.

Max was so busy carving sheep and making money that he gave scant thought to romance. But at age 42, he met a woman half his age who married him, if truth be told, for his money. She got none of it, for twelve months later she died in childbirth, leaving behind a blond-haired, blue-eyed daughter named Johanna.

Max, however, was effectively distracted from the joy and grief of it all by his work. A popular American magazine devoted its December issue to "The Man Who Traded Wool for Wood." So Max found himself jetting to New York, to Chicago, to Seattle, to Orlando, to London, to Vienna, giving interviews, signing autographs, and making more money. A special showing of Schroeder originals opened in a small, but superb museum in Windsor, and Max, amid popping flashbulbs, presented one of his carvings to the Prince of Wales himself. *Newsweek* did a story.

Max's bank account grew, and Schroeder Sheep found their way into the world's most exclusive stores.

Max was in his sixties when Johanna found him slumped over his workbench. It was his heart. His recovery was both slow and depressing, and for the first time in fifty years, Max lost interest in his work.

"But you absolutely must not give up, Father," Johanna said every morning. "Jason and I are going to give you a grandchild, and you mustn't die before he's born. He is due in December."

And Max, looking up from his bed was surprised at how beautifully comforting Johanna's face was. He had never before taken enough time to study his daughter's face. He had never realized how fair her skin or how blue her eyes. They twinkled and sparkled even when yielding an occasional tear. She proved a good nurse, and within weeks Max was able to sit in his chair. His tools, however, lay forgotten, his carvings untouched, his craving for fame and money diminished.

Kasper was born on his grandfather's sixty-fifth Christmas, arriving thumb in mouth. When Johanna placed the baby in her father's arms, the old man's artist-eye missed nothing. He had never felt such softness or sensed such love. Nor had he ever seen such created perfection. The baby's one hand was balled into a tiny fist to be sucked on. The miniature fingers of the other hand gripped the tip of the granddad's little finger like a vice.

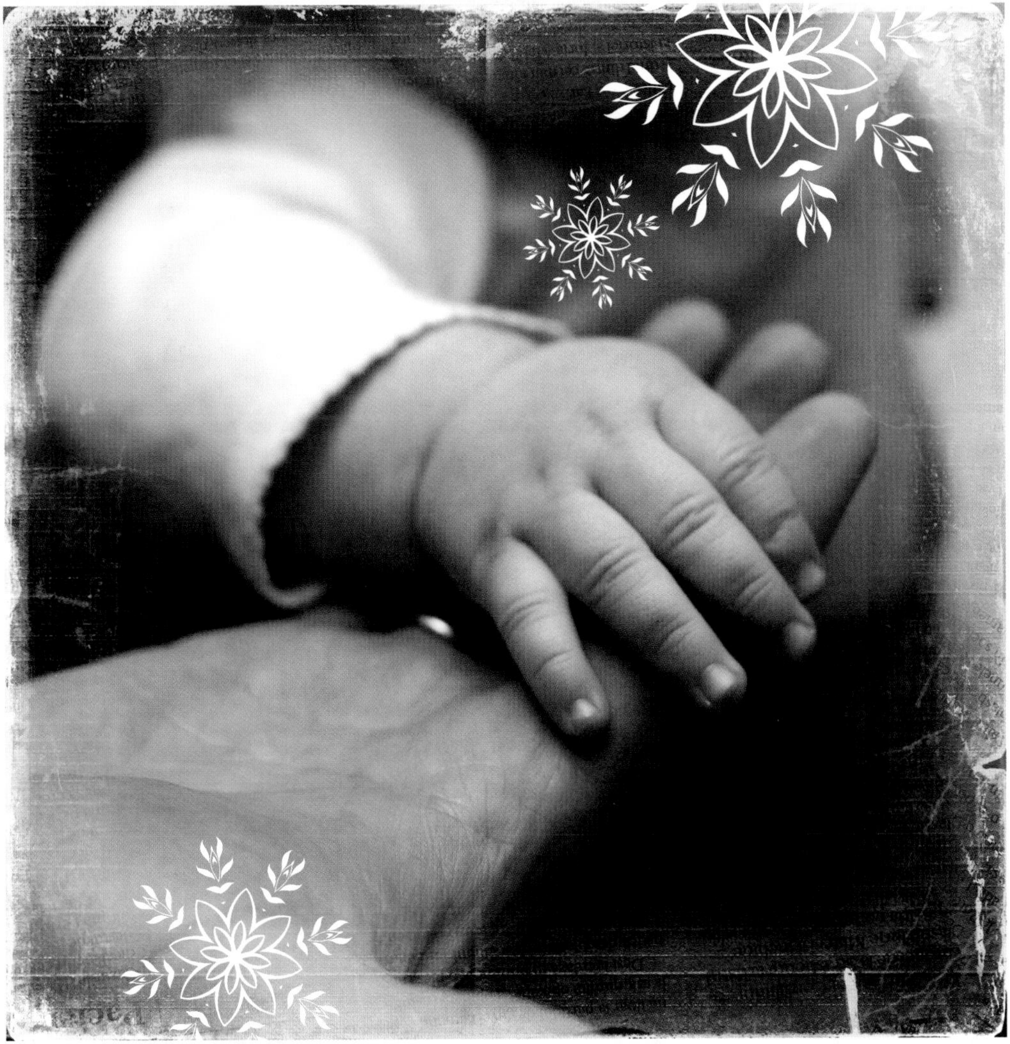

The parish priest arrived at dusk, stomping his feet on the stoop to dislodge the snow. Father Christopher, vicar of St. Joseph's Chapel, was one of those unfortunate people who appear thirty years older than they really are. His face was a spider's web of lines, but each line communicated character. His hair was as white and thin as the cirrus clouds over the Alps. His voice was as clear as a yodeler's call.

Max liked him, and the two struck up a friendship. At Father Christopher's suggestion, the craftsman began reading his New Testament, soon coming to Luke 2.

On the very morning he read the Christmas story—New Year's Day—Max received Father Christopher for coffee. "Why have I never loved this story before?" asked Max. "Why have I never carved Christmas sheep, nor the shepherds watching their flocks by night?"

"Ah," said the priest. "It is because you have so loved the sheep of Switzerland, that you have missed the Lamb of God."

"I have been a selfish man," Max confessed. "I have lived for idols of wood. Now I shall live for the Lord Christ. And if the Lord Christ will but strengthen me, I shall create something wonderful for the Great Shepherd whose sheep I have duplicated all my life."

Then taking his checkbook, Max wrote a check. With one slash of his pen, he gave away exactly one-fourth of his fortune. St. Joseph's Chapel was endowed. A new heating system was installed, the old roof was replaced, the organ repaired, the exterior cleaned of a century of blackening soot, and a small elevator installed for the disabled.

Furthermore, Bibles were placed in all the hotels of Zurich and Lucerne, an orphanage in Ghana was underwritten, and a Swiss missionary in Costa Rica received a new Land Rover.

Shortly afterward, on January 6, Epiphany, Max woke up feeling that his vigor had returned. "I shall go back to my work today," he announced. For the first time in months, his rugged hands caressed his tools and picked up his neglected wood. By day's end, he had carved a lamb—not a Swiss lamb, but a Judean one. It was larger than most lambs he had ever crafted . . . and more beautiful. Every tuft of wool, each blackened hoof, the rounded ears and glistening nose, the beholding eyes, it was all unequaled. The piece seemed to live. Max almost expected to hear it bleat.

Next came a shepherd with a kindly face etched with lines like a spider's web. Then came Mary, with eyes that seemed to twinkle and sparkle, even as a tear ran down her cheek. Then came a sleeping infant, left thumb in mouth, right hand gripping the tip of Mary's little finger like a vice. There followed nine other pieces.

It was a crèche only a heartbeat away from life itself, and all who saw it knew that it was Max Schroeder's masterpiece. When *Newsweek* featured it on the cover of its overseas edition the following Christmas, requests for copies came from all over the world. Collectors, craving it for their displays, offered up to a million Swiss francs. Museums and churches sent curators begging for it.

The answer was always the same. "You shall have it," said Max with a forbearing smile, "over my dead body."

The toughest requests came from family and friends. Johanna hinted. Father Christopher gazed at it wistfully. And young Kasper asked for it outright with childlike simplicity.

"Ah," said Max Schroeder, a friendly glint in his eye, "and you shall have it—over my dead body."

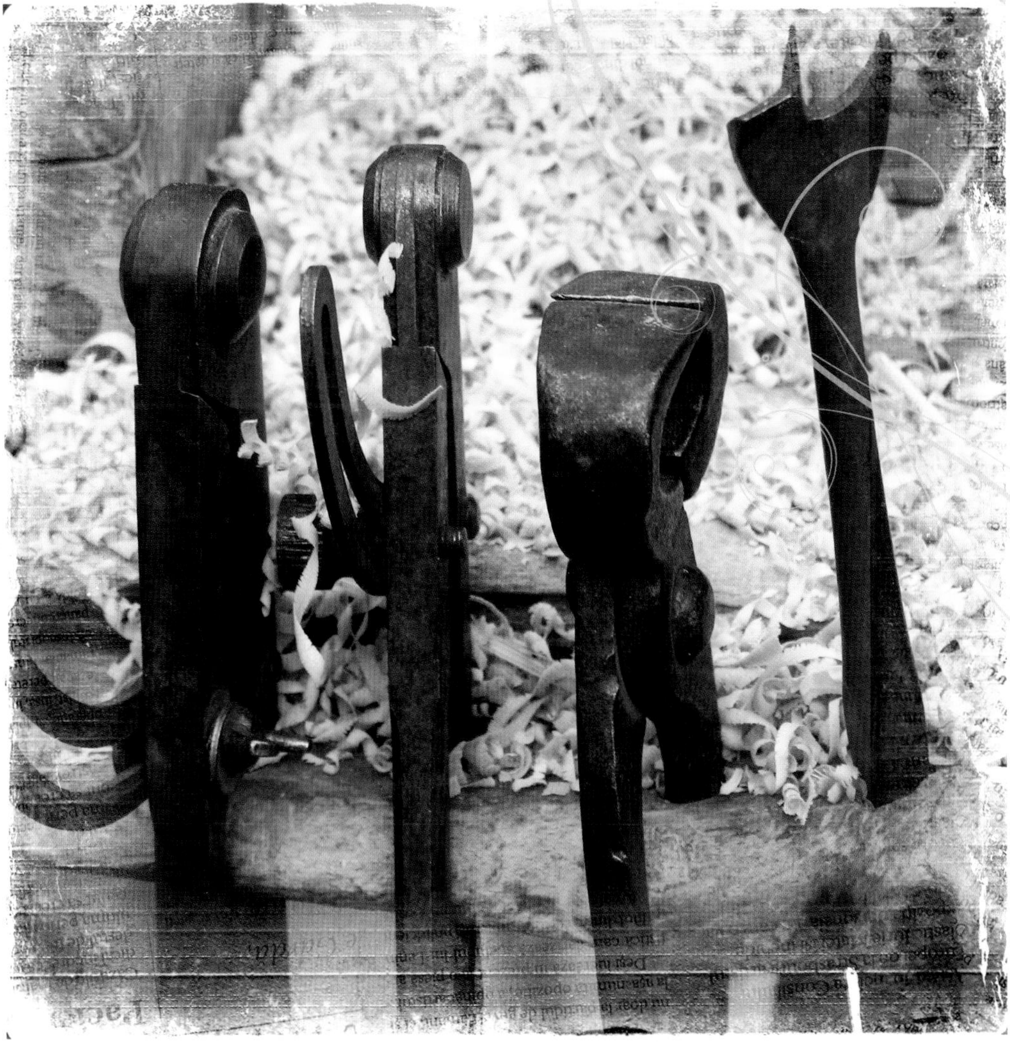

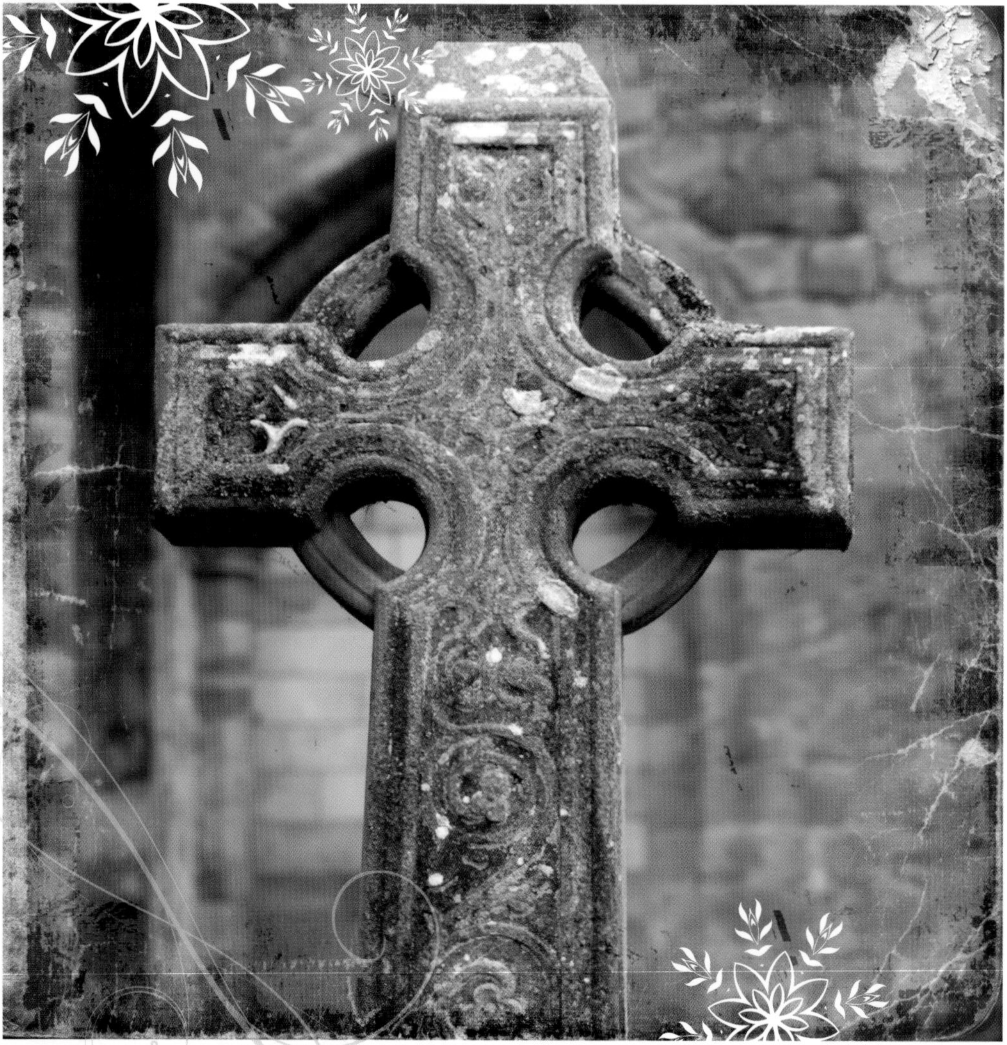

Max's second heart attack took him suddenly in his seventy-ninth year, and all Lucerne turned out for his funeral. In recognition of his tender generosity, he was buried in classic European fashion, under the floor of the church he had endowed, beneath the cobbled stones on which the altar table rested.

Following the funeral, friends gathered for the reading of his will. His money and possessions were allocated as expected, to family and church. There were no surprises, nor had any been expected for Max had explained his wishes in advance. The only uncertainty lay with the nativity. To whom did Max Schroeder leave the bright-eyed Mary, the thumb-sucking Christ child, the nearly bleating sheep, the web-faced shepherd?

To Johanna, who had nursed him to health? To Kasper, his only grandchild? To Father Christopher, who had brought him new life? To a great museum where thousands would see it?

In the end, he left it to all of them—by leaving it to none of them.

"And my nativity I leave to my dear church house, St. Joseph's Chapel, where I lately learned to worship the Great Shepherd, to be displayed every Christmas season until the Christ child Himself shall return."

And so it is that every Christmas, the parishioners of little St. Joseph's Chapel on the edge of Lake Lucerne may see Max Schroeder's crèche with its thumb-sucking Christ child, arranged simply and beautifully on the altar table—over his dead body.

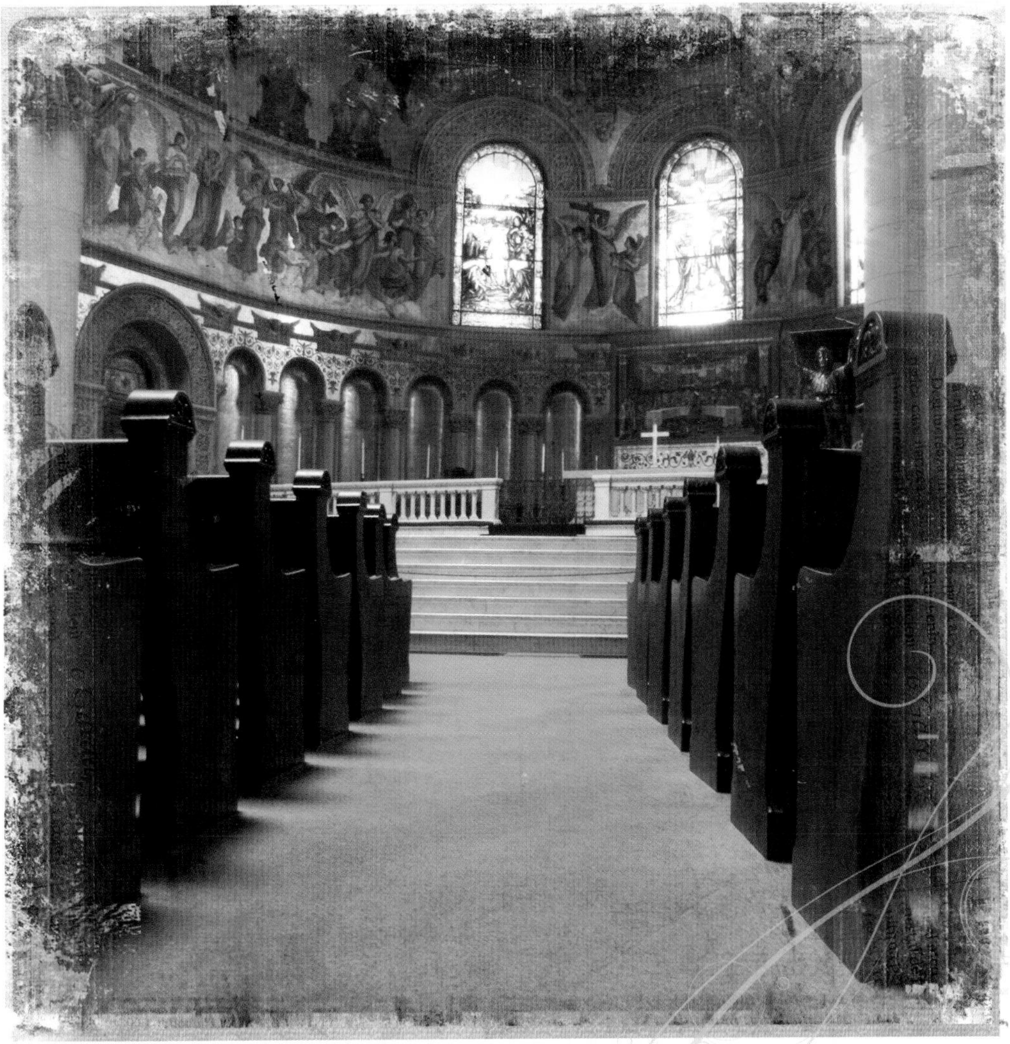

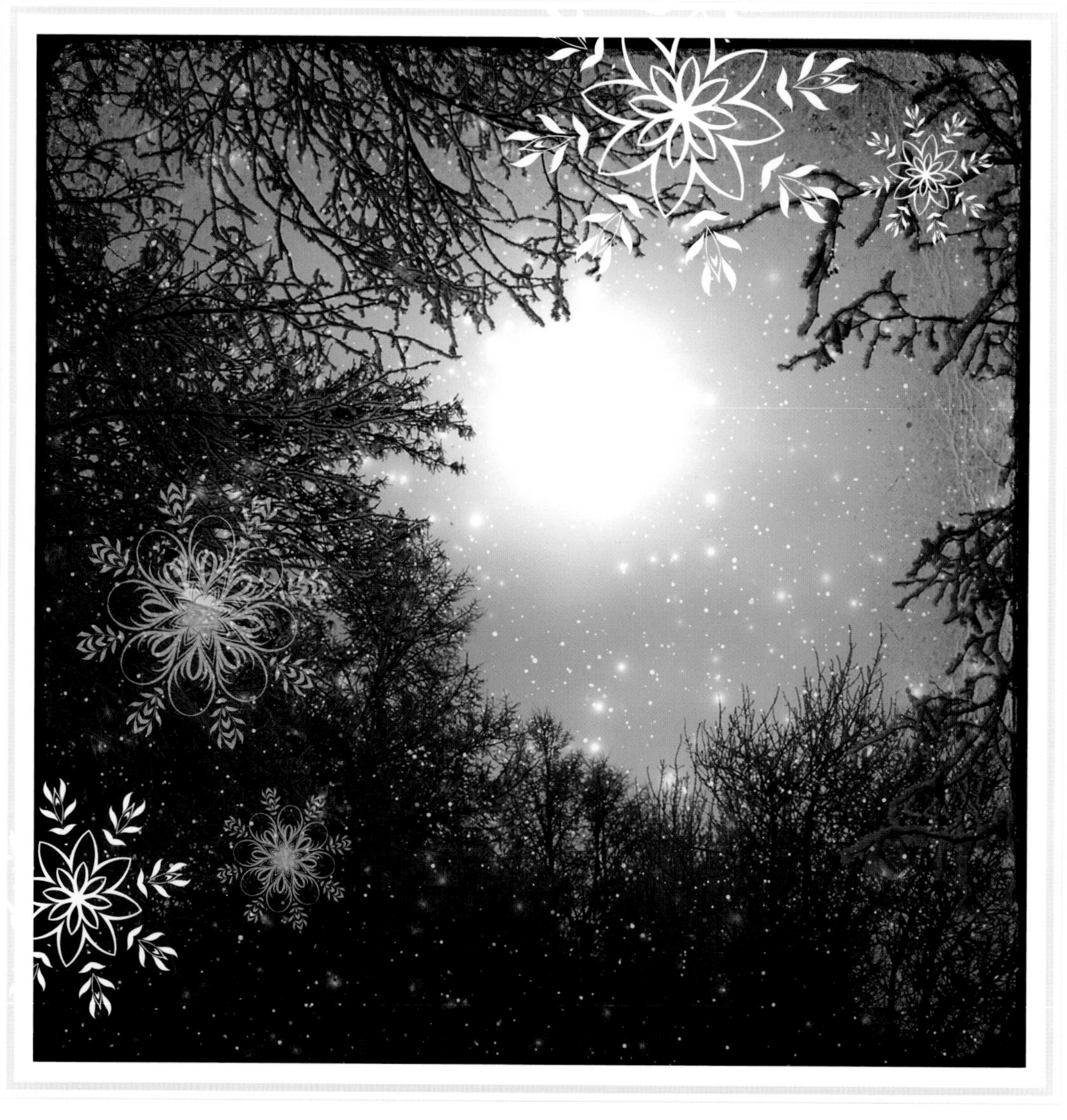

Five-Quarters of a Mile

he old man had never seen such weather. The Appalachians were blanketed with enough snow to bury the mountain roads, not to mention the cow paths snaking along the hills and the sheds tottering in the fields. Life was at a standstill. Even the snowbirds huddled away in unseen boroughs, unwilling to break the stillness of the forbidding freeze.

Old Zeek arched his feet and stood on his toes, looking through the top pane of his kitchen window. The snow had drifted to eye-level, and he was anxious. He didn't mind being alone in the mountains, but he didn't like being *trapped* here, not one bit, especially with his feeling poorly *and* his being responsible for a six-year-old.

Zeek had enough food in the cupboard and enough firewood on the hillside; that was no problem. But if something happened to him . . . well, he was stranded, that's all there was to it. Stranded with a young child in an old house, the two of them practically buried alive in a snowstorm, the likes of which he'd never seen.

Zeek Miller—short for Ezekiel he guessed, though he'd never been anything but Zeek—lived in an unpainted frame house at the head of a hollow, five-quarters of a mile from the nearest two-lane road. There wasn't a neighbor within hollerin' distance. Until now, that had been just fine. Zeek took a likin' to people well enough, but he liked being alone too. His wife was long gone, swept away in the flu epidemic of 1918. He'd raised Lawrence by himself. Now with Lawrence working up North, Zeek was keeping his grandson, Adam, until better times came.

Adam was a chip off the old block. He loved the mountains like his grandpa, and Zeek figured he'd one day inherit the old farm. They were buddies, the two of them. They hiked down the mountain every Sunday for church, every Wednesday for groceries, and whenever Zeek had some produce to sell.

Zeek grew vegetables at forty-degree angles on the mountain slopes. He had a small herd of goats he milked for money, but he'd long ago given up the cow, the horse, and all the other critters, except for an old hen that lived under the porch of his little cabin. He was getting tired and didn't want a lot of things to look after.

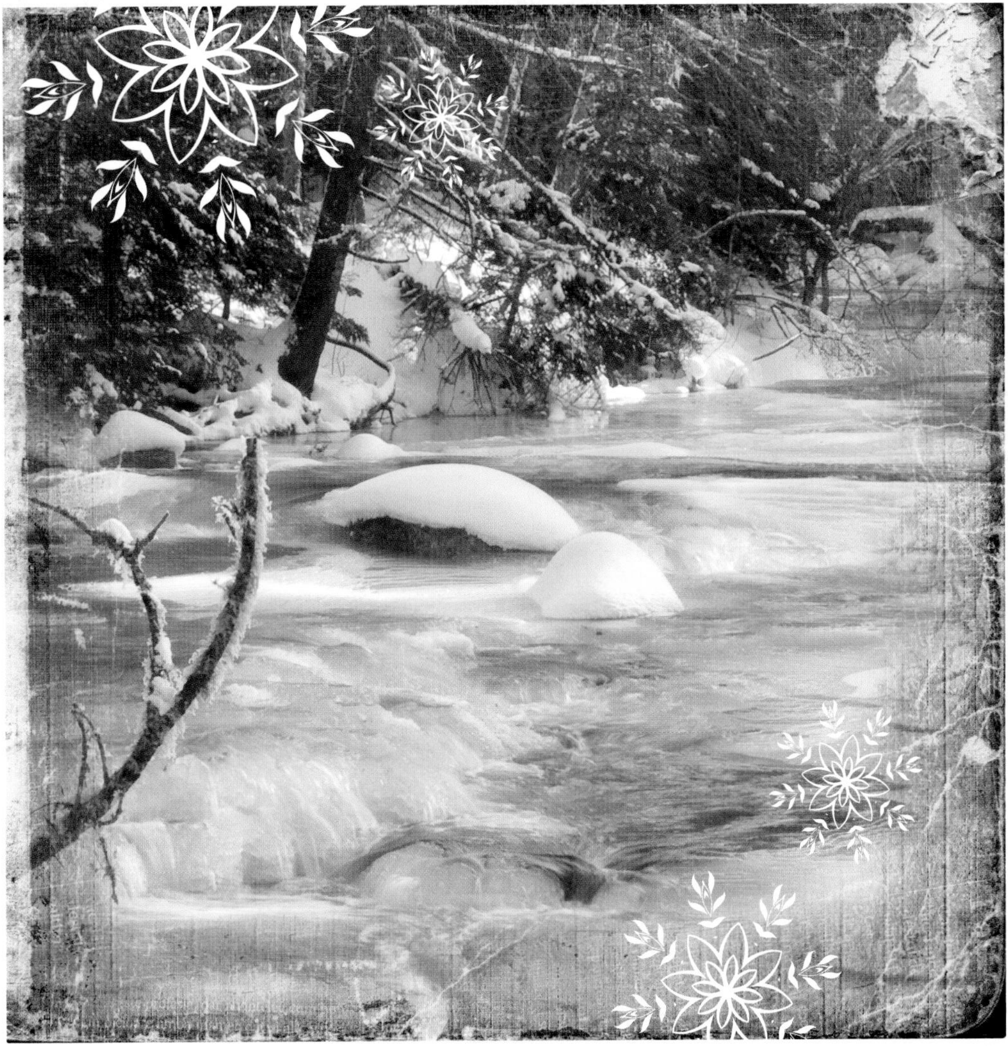

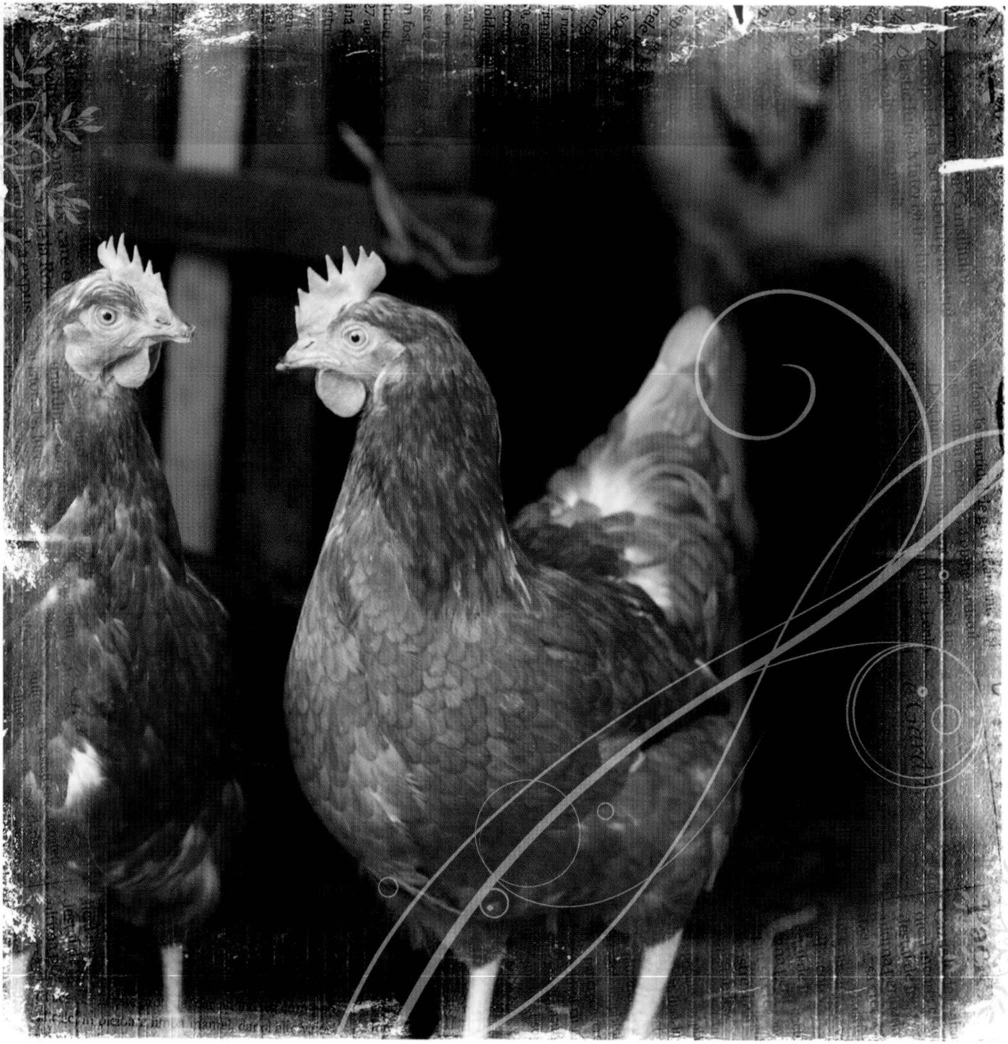

"Reckon we're stuck here sure enough, Grandpa," said Adam, climbing onto the kitchen counter and peering through the top of the window. "Reckon Pa ain't gonna make it home for Christmas, after all."

"No, boy . . . ain't nary a chance."

"Wish he hadn't gone off like that," said Adam, for the hundredth time. "What with Ma dead and all; I wish he hadn't gone north. Wish he'd just come back. Wish he'd be here tomorrow for Christmas. But I reckon he ain't gonna come, is he?"

"Well, boy, you know he's a'tryin'," said Zeek. "Wishin's good, but it don't make things happen. This Depression, son, it's wonderful bad. There ain't no work here, no way t'make a living. I told you that a'fore. Your daddy's got hisself a job up there in Ohio, and he's sendin' us money every week. That's why you got shoes on your feet. Now, he's gonna be here if he can git hisself here, that's for certain. But this snow, son, this is a true, honest-to-goodness blizzard, that's what it is. Now, you fetch me a match, boy. It's gettin' dark, and I reckon we best light the lamp."

Adam scrambled off the counter and ran to the matchbox on the wall. "I'm getting' cold again, Grandpa," he said, returning match in hand.

"Yeah, me too, Adam," said the old man, striking the match and lighting the wick of the old lantern. The clock on the wall struck five times, and Zeek, glancing at it, thought of supper. "After I fetch us some more firewood, son, I'll stir us up some grub. Just look at that wood box. It's 'bout near empty again, and I just filled it at lunchtime. Reckon I'd best try to fill it up before it's plumb dark outside."

"I'll help you, Grandpa."

"No, boy, you best stay in. It's too cold for a child to be out a'doors. You'd nigh freeze t'death. You listen for me and, when I holler, you open the door real wide and let me back in. I'll have m'hands full."

Zeek's old boots, cracked with age, sat by the door, and it took him a while to stuff his feet into them and lace the strings. He shoved his arms into his tattered wool coat, then pulled his cap over his thick, gray hair. When he opened the door, a freezing gust rattled the house and made him shudder. Ducking outside, Zeek banged the door behind him and trudged through the dusk toward the woodpile.

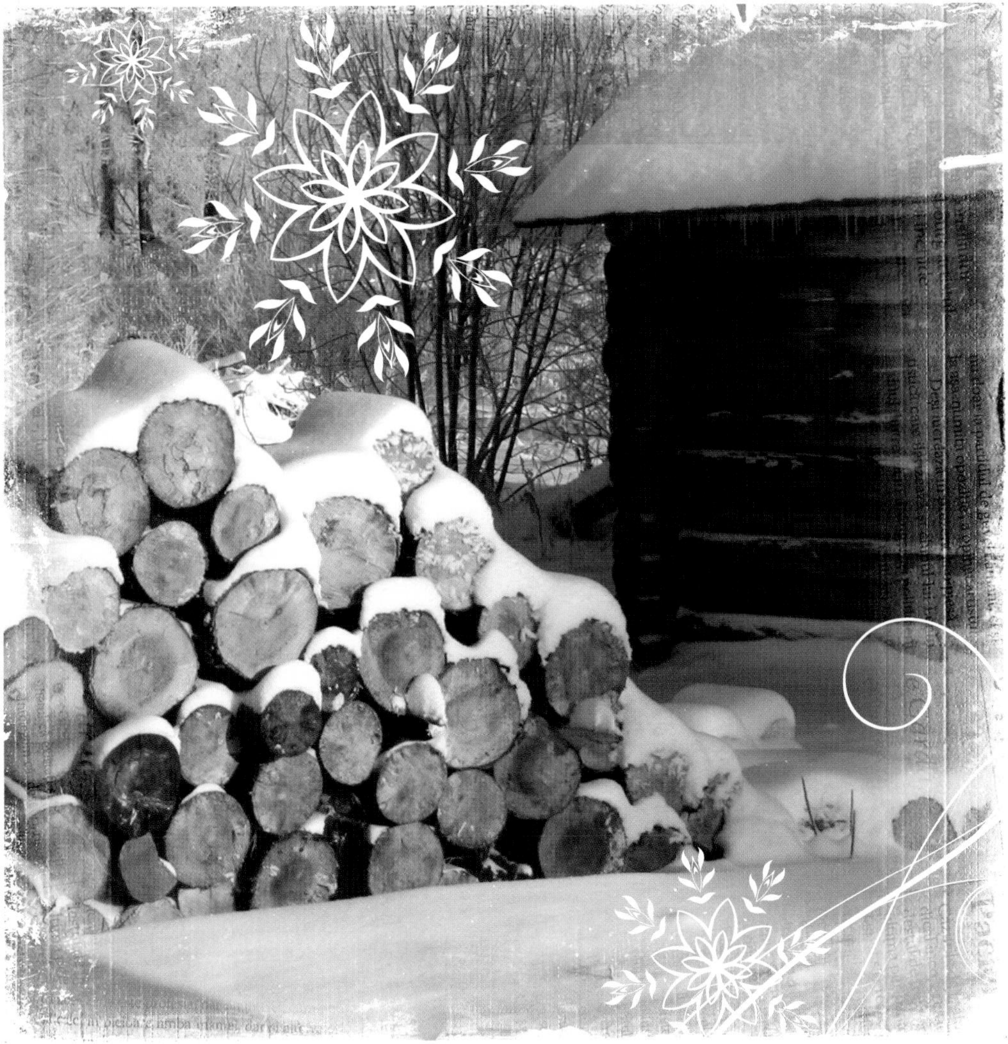

He knew why the firewood was burning so quickly, and it bothered him. The wood was too dry. He'd been stopping at the upper end of the woodpile and carting last year's wood back to the house, and it was so dry it burned like paper. The box by the stove emptied as fast as he filled it. But the old wood was lighter, and Zeek was having trouble carrying the heavier wood.

That worried him. He'd always worked like a horse and, even at seventy-six, he was hale and hearty, or so he thought. He'd been gathering firewood for seven decades, and he knew fire logs like a scholar knows history.

But something was wrong, and Zeek felt winter in his bones. Two days ago, he'd had a spell while shoveling snow from the path that led past the woodpile and on to the outhouse. That pathway was crucial. "We don't have to go to town," he'd explained to Adam. "We don't even have to go to the church house; but we do have to git to the firewood and down to the outhouse. Those are the 'portant things—the firewood and the outhouse. Gotta keep a path open, or we'll be in real trouble."

But his path clearing had exacted a heavy price, and Zeek had been sick to his stomach and sore in his chest ever since. His arms felt weak, and he winced with a catch in his lungs. His breath was labored, and as he trudged to the woodpile, he tried to veer down toward the newer wood. But his feet slipped beneath him; and he found himself standing at the upper end where he selected an armful of dryer, lighter wood. Four sticks and that just about did it. He couldn't lift another piece.

Approaching the house, Zeek took a deep breath and called as loudly as he could, "Adam! Open the door." The pain struck his chest like a bullet, hitting him point blank, slicing through his flesh, into his lungs, through his heart. His legs gave way. Firewood tumbled onto his head, and he tried to break his fall with one hand, clutching his chest with the other. The dusk turned to darkness, and a paralyzing cold fell on him like an avalanche....

Somewhere in his unconsciousness, Zeek felt he was drowning in a frozen lake, high in the mountains, swimming upward toward the ice that covered the surface. Finally he broke through the water and through the ice, and he opened his eyes. Adam peered down at him anxiously with red eyes and a face as white as the snow that surrounded them.

"What happened?" Zeek asked, wincing as pain shot through him like circuits of fire.

"You fell something awful, Grandpa," said Adam. "I like to a'never pulled you through the door."

"How long ago?" said Zeek, struggling with every word. He tried to lift himself onto his elbow, but couldn't. "How long have I been like this?"

"A might spell," said Adam. "I've just been a'sittin' here beside you. But, Grandpa, the firewood's nearly gone, and it's gettin' mighty cold."

Zeek lifted his head. It was dark now, the only light being the flickering flame of the oil lamp casting deep shadows that quivered on the walls. Suddenly the gears on the old clock moved and the striker hit the coils. One . . . two . . . three . . . and on to ten. Ten o'clock, and cold.

"That firewood you brought, I got it outta the snow. I've been puttin' it in the stove, but it's gone now," said Adam, "and the fire's 'bout out. I reckon I'd best go and get us some more wood."

"No," said Zeek, wheezing, speaking with labored breaths. "No, Adam, you can't; it's too dark . . . too bad . . . cold. Might not make it back. If you git lost, you'd freeze yourself to death."

"But, Grandpa, there's a path. You dug it for us."

"Ya can't go out there," said Zeek. "The woodpile, it's too far. It's icy. You might fall, might not make it back . . . git lost . . . too dark . . . it's cold . . ."

"But, Grandpa, we're gonna freeze in here. We gotta keep the fire a'goin'."

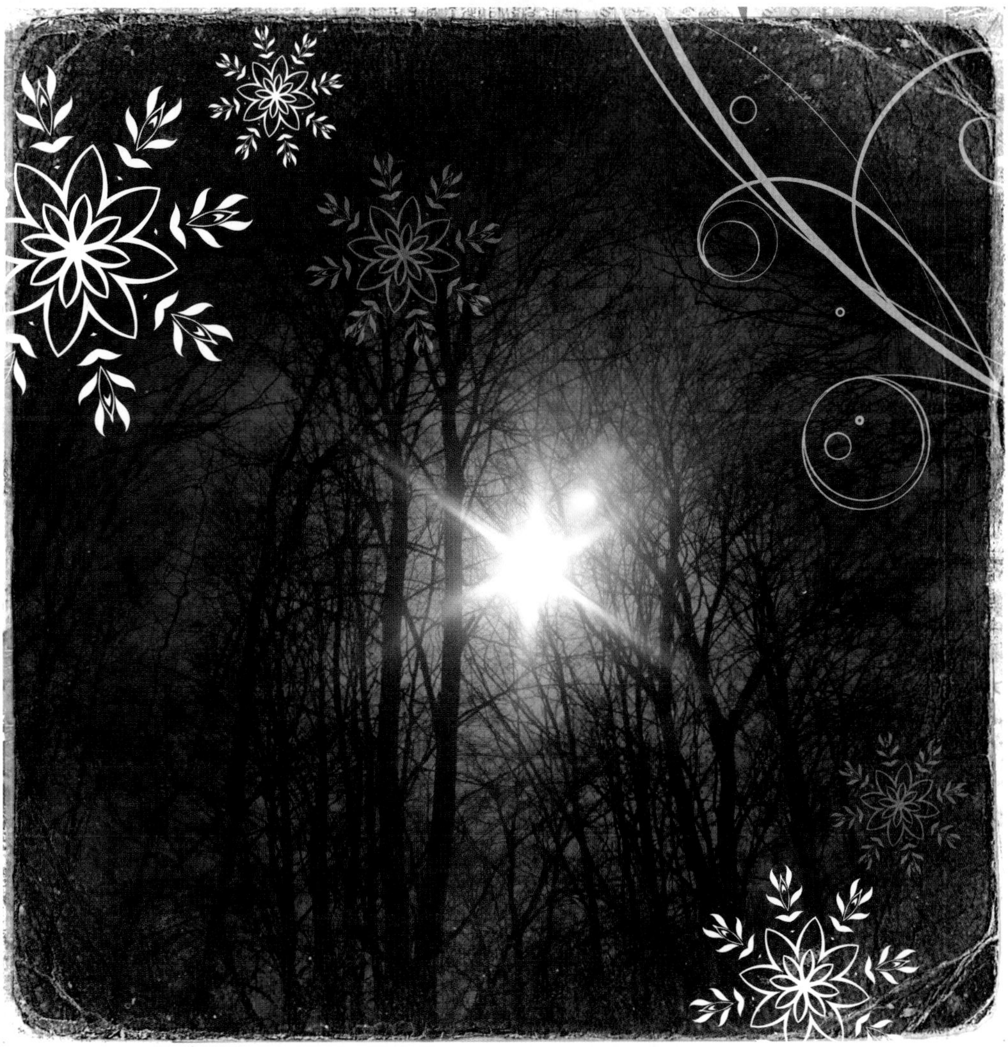

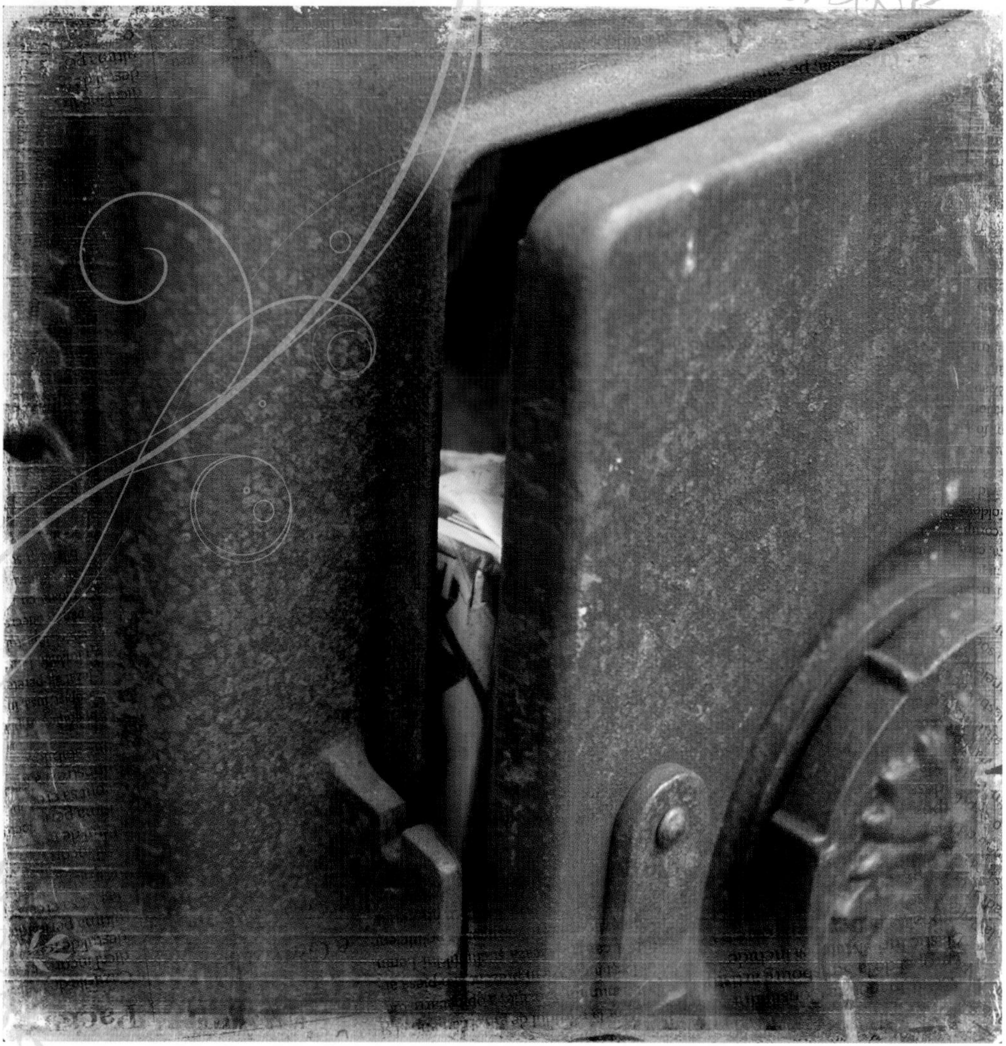

Zeek's head dropped back onto the floor. The pain was running down his arms, but the boy was right. If the fire went out, they'd freeze before morning. But if the boy went out, he'd freeze before midnight. Zeek closed his eyes and prayed for help.

"Adam," he said at last, "Adam, burn the kings."

"What, Grandpa?"

"Those three kings over there. Go get 'em. Throw 'em in the stove, one at a time. Go on, you gotta do it now before the fire goes out."

Adam glanced to the large nativity in the corner of the room, shrouded in the shadows. Each piece was made of hickory and was about a foot tall, about the size of a piece of firewood. Zeek's grandfather had whittled the pieces out many years ago, one per winter, until the entire set had been finished. The wood was well seasoned and heavy, and was the closest thing Zeek had to an heirloom. For many years, he'd made a little display in the corner of the flowerbed during Christmas. But this year the snow had come early, so he'd hauled the figures from the barn and set them in the corner of his little room.

"Grandpa, you love those ol' kings. We can't burn 'em."

Zeek, grimacing with pain, lifted himself up on an elbow to look the boy in the eyes. "Now you listen to me real good. You take and haul those kings to the stove and throw them on the fire, one at a time. You've got to do it, Adam, right now before the fire goes plumb out."

Without another word, Adam obeyed. Zeek sunk back onto the floor and drifted into unconsciousness. The next time he opened his eyes, the clock was striking twelve times. Midnight. Adam was curled next to him asleep, an old blanket spread over the two. Using one hand, Zeek shook the boy. "Adam, wake up. Adam! You've got to tend the fire again."

"What's that, Grandpa?"

"Adam, throw the sheep on the fire. Do it now, Adam. It's getting colder."

Adam rubbed his eyes, rolled over onto his feet, padded to the corner, and like a heartless shepherd threw the innocent lambs into the stove, arranging them with the poker. He watched a few minutes as the wood slowly caught fire, casting off a heat that baked him in delicious warmth.

At two o'clock, the three shepherds went into the furnace, one at a time—like Shadrach, Meshach, and Abednego, but without a Fourth Man to deliver them.

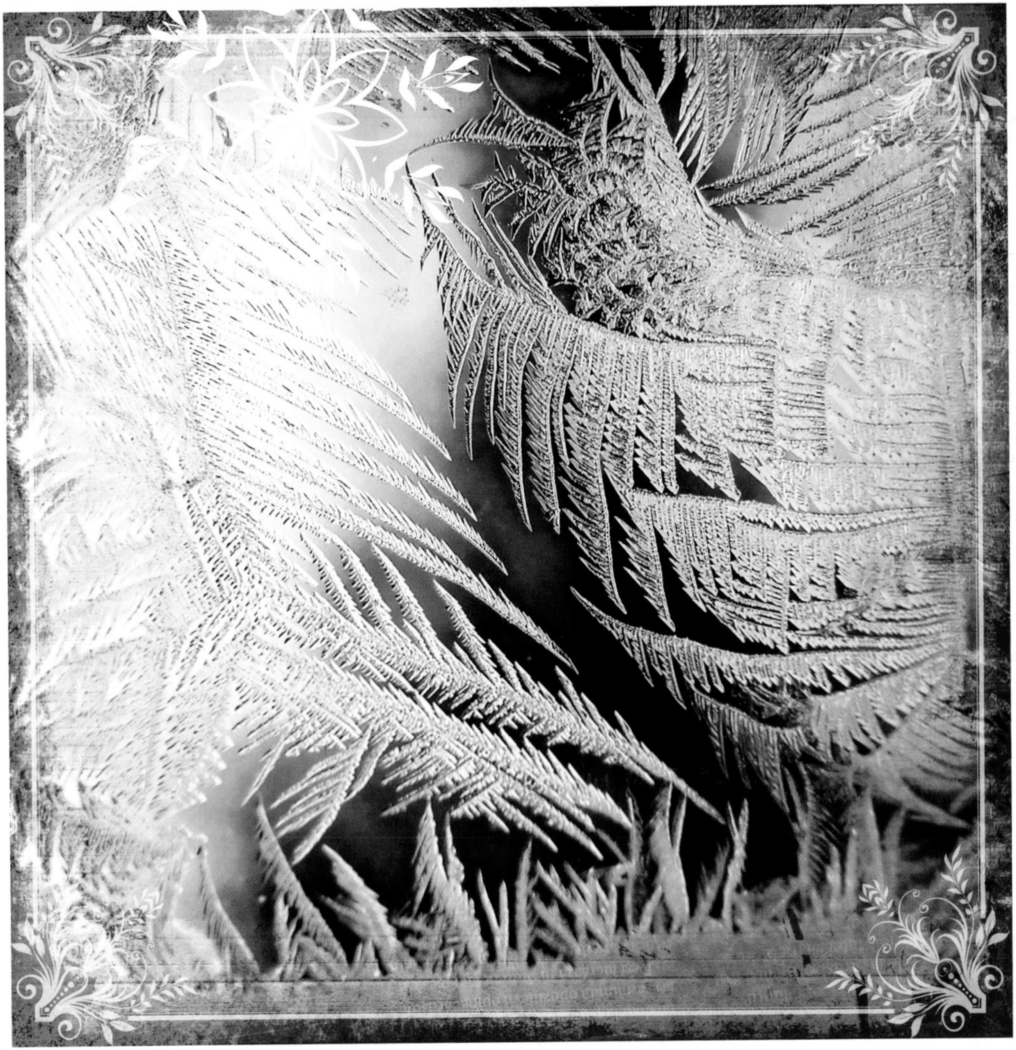

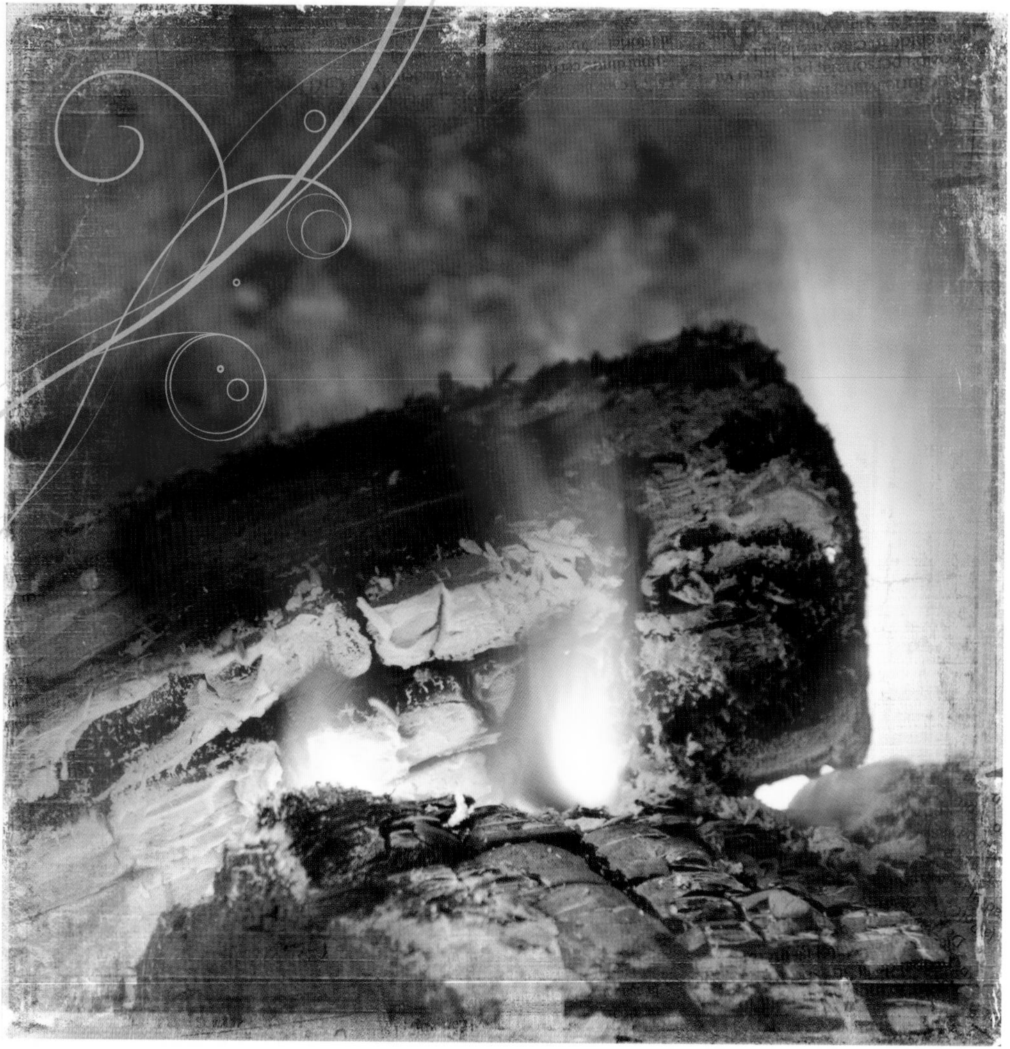

When the clock struck four, Zeek again shook his grandson awake, this time to throw Joseph onto the fire. Fortunately, Joseph was a portly fellow of unusually hard hickory, and it took him a while to give up the ghost. But by six o'clock, it was Mary's turn to be consigned to the flames.

By seven o'clock, the sun was coming up, but it was a bitter morning and the fire was nearly out. Into the stove went the manger. Now only the Christ child remained, like a lone figure lying on the floor in the corner of the room, the sole survivor of the night's holocaust. Adam fetched some bread and milk, and Zeek nibbled it before giving the final order.

"Adam," he said, "throw baby Jesus in the stove."

"But, Grandpa . . ."

"Just do it, Adam."

Adam loved the baby Jesus, and this Christmas he had plucked him off his manager every day to hold him and play with him. Jesus was smaller than the other figures and easier to manage. His figure was so personal and lifelike, and the expression on his face was so strong and happy. Adam opened the door and as carefully as he could, trying not to burn himself, he gently placed Jesus on the hot coals. The poker remained propped against the wall, for Adam knew he couldn't jab at this piece. The baby's eyes peered back at him from the glowing enclosure of the old stove, lying not in a manger of hay, but on a bed of embers.

"Sorry 'bout this," Adam whispered, closing and latching the door. It was done. The flames started to lick the wood like a serpent, and soon Jesus was ablaze in the flames of the old stove. Adam felt a tear slide down his cheek as he turned away. He ran to his grandpa, still lying on the floor, buried his face in the old man's chest, and cried, not only for Jesus, but for his grandpa whose face had never seemed so old or wrinkled or gray.

"It's gonna be alright," said old Zeek, lifting his hand to stroke the boy's hair. "Baby Jesus is gonna save us, you just see. Just think of the heat and the light he's giving right now." Zeek closed his eyes and his hand rested silently on the boy's hair.

❄ ❄ ❄

Zeek's next conscious thought was hearing the gear of the clock wind up to strike again. This time he was unable to count the strokes, and when he tried to open his eyes, his vision was blurred. But he felt linens around him, a mattress under his bones, and a pillow beneath his head.

A large hand seemed to be squeezing his own, and a deep, familiar voice fell on his ears.

"'Bout time you stirred, Pop. Git those eyes of your'n open. I'm heatin' ya some goat's milk. You know how that settles your stomach. It's Christmas Day. Adam, fetch me that glass of milk for Pop."

Zeek felt a hand lift his head and a glass touch his lips. He took a sip as best he could. The voice continued, "I've been here a while, but I walked back down to the highway and sent for the doctor. He'll be comin' directly, I reckon. You're gonna be alright. I've got the fire goin' real big; it's nice and warm in here, and you'll be fine."

Zeek opened his eyes a little wider and tried to speak. A soft smile flickered then faded on his weathered face, and he closed his eyes to rest a spell.

After Christmas that winter I returned with my dad to Ohio, leaving my grandpa under the deep mid-winter's snow of his Tennessee mountains. His old place lay dormant and abandoned for many years, but not forgotten. Now I've returned, for my life has come full circle. Many winters have passed since that cold Christmas long ago, but I often relive the never-to-be-forgotten night, five-quarters of a mile into the hills, when the Christmas story went up in flames and the Christ child perished in the fire to save my life.

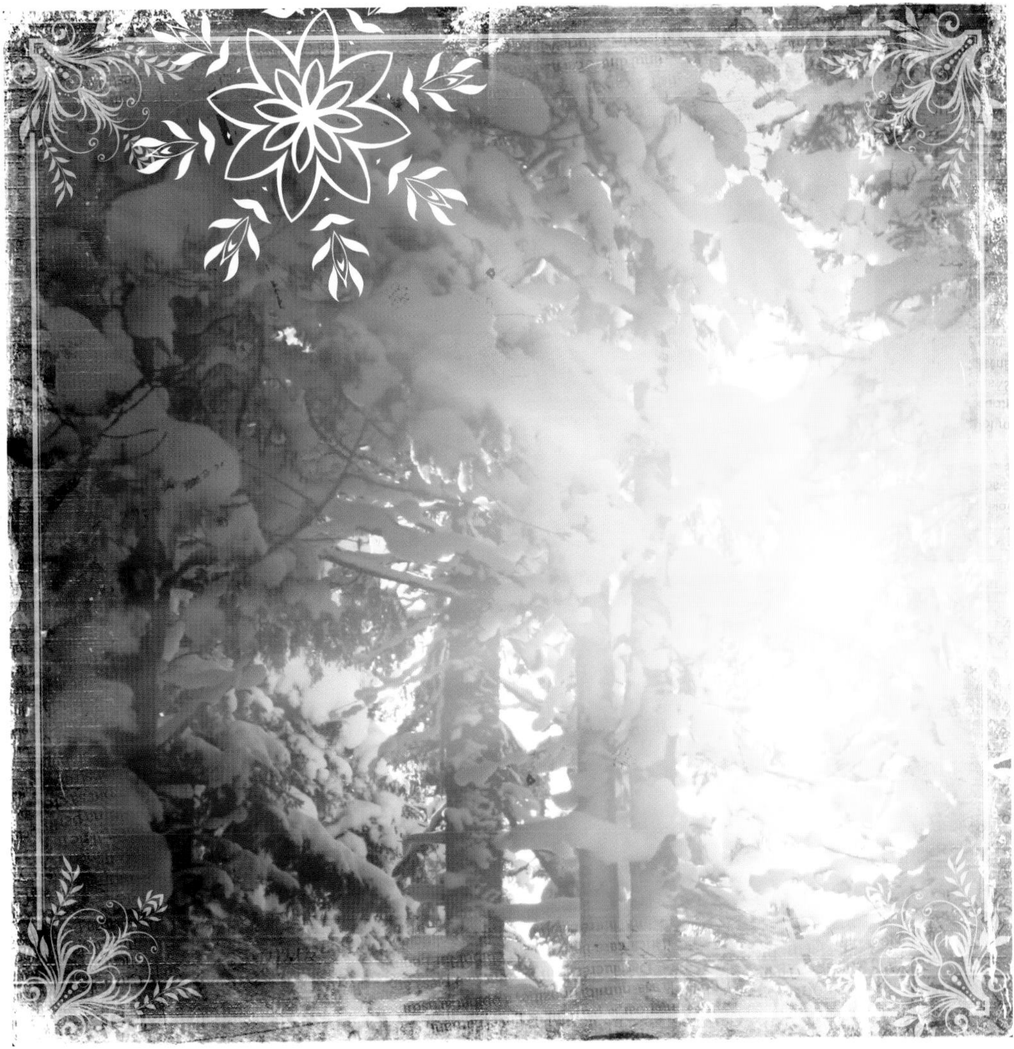

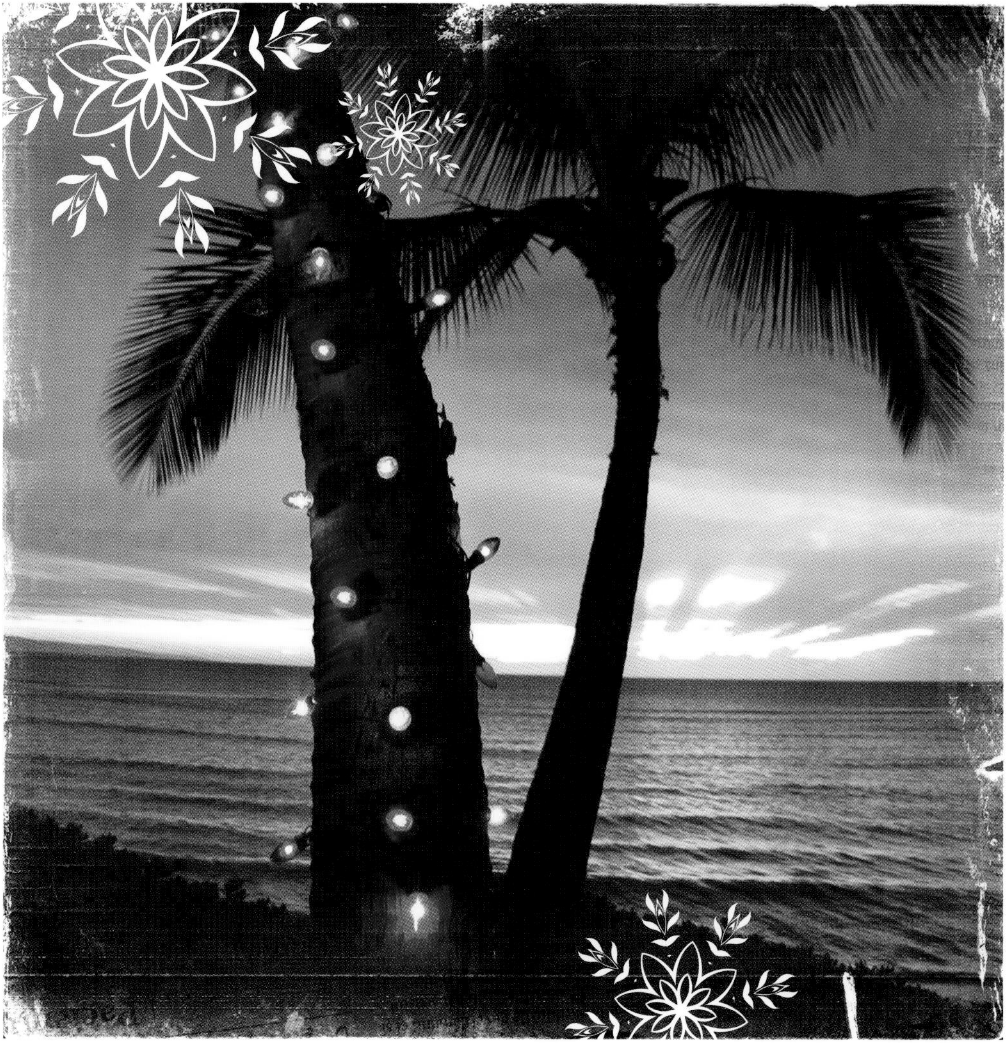

Nativity Seen Smiling

amon never wanted a big December wedding, but Claire, spurred on by her mother, had insisted. And Claire had never wanted to go to Puerto Rico for their honeymoon, but Damon's travel agent friend had given them the four-day trip as a wedding present—and Damon, never one to pass up a bargain, had insisted.

And so, wilted and weary beyond words, the nervous couple had dashed from the wedding to the airport for the red-eye from Denver to Miami, then raced to the connecting flight from Miami to San Juan, and finally were driven by overpriced taxi to Old San Juan itself.

They arrived irritably at midmorning to find their room at the Hotel Presidente still occupied by the previous guest. While waiting in the lobby, Claire drank a large glass of pulpy orange juice—which contained sixteen ounces of something lasting 36 to 48 hours. She was instantly good for nothing but the bathroom.

A frustrated Damon had spent the afternoon napping at the pool. His fair, un-lotioned skin had broiled in the Puerto Rican sun, and the resulting blisters had left him so sore he could barely be touched.

The unhappy couple had snapped at each other endlessly, taken their meals in silence, and thwarted all efforts at honeymoon bliss. Even their tour of the Puerto Rican rain forest had been a washout. Now they were down to their last day.

"It was a terrible mistake," Damon muttered, standing in his boxers by the window during a sudden downpour.

"The trip?" asked Claire.

"Yes," said Damon. "The trip. The wedding. The whole thing. I'm not saying I don't love you, but we couldn't have started things worse. I'm still exhausted from that wedding your mother staged. The grand ballroom, three photographers, five hundred guests, two hundred poinsettias, and a Colorado Supreme Court justice. I'm still a bundle of nerves about that. Nothing was missing except the partridge in the pear tree."

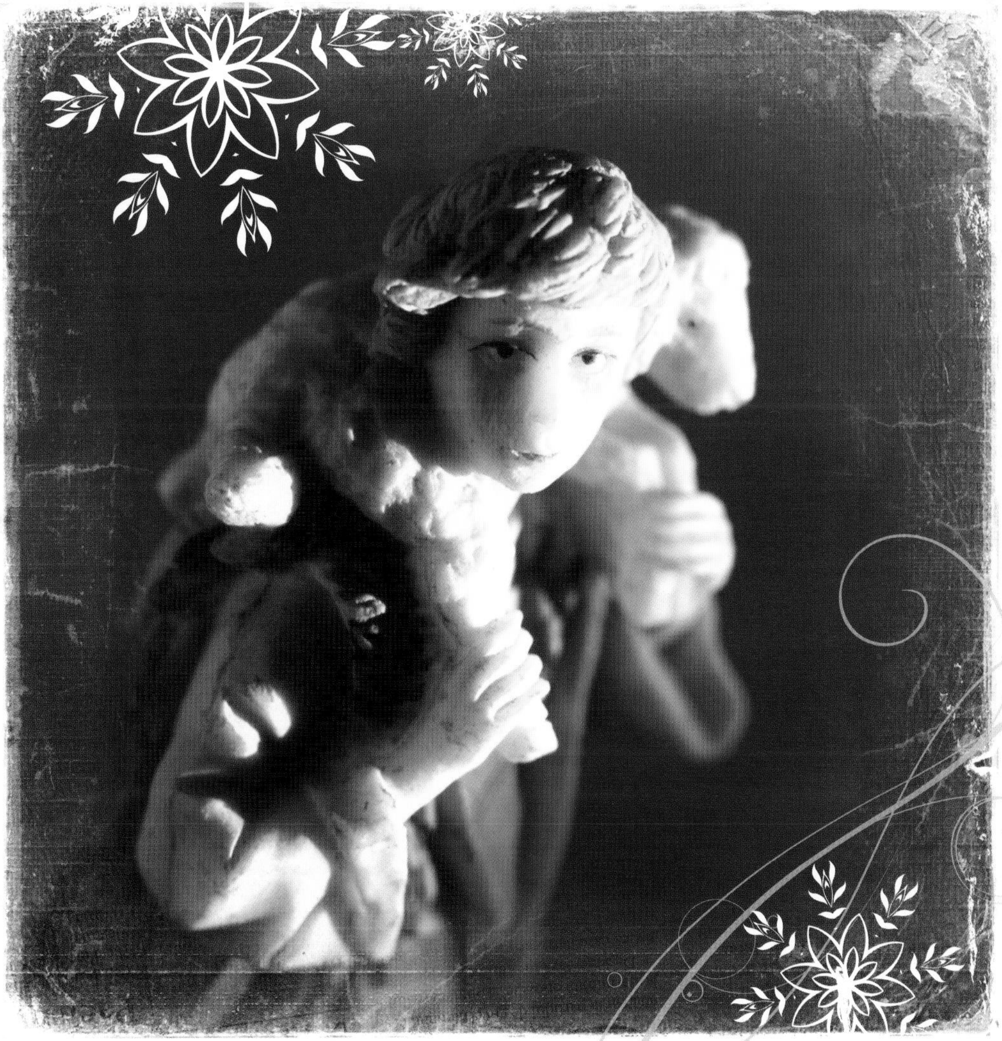

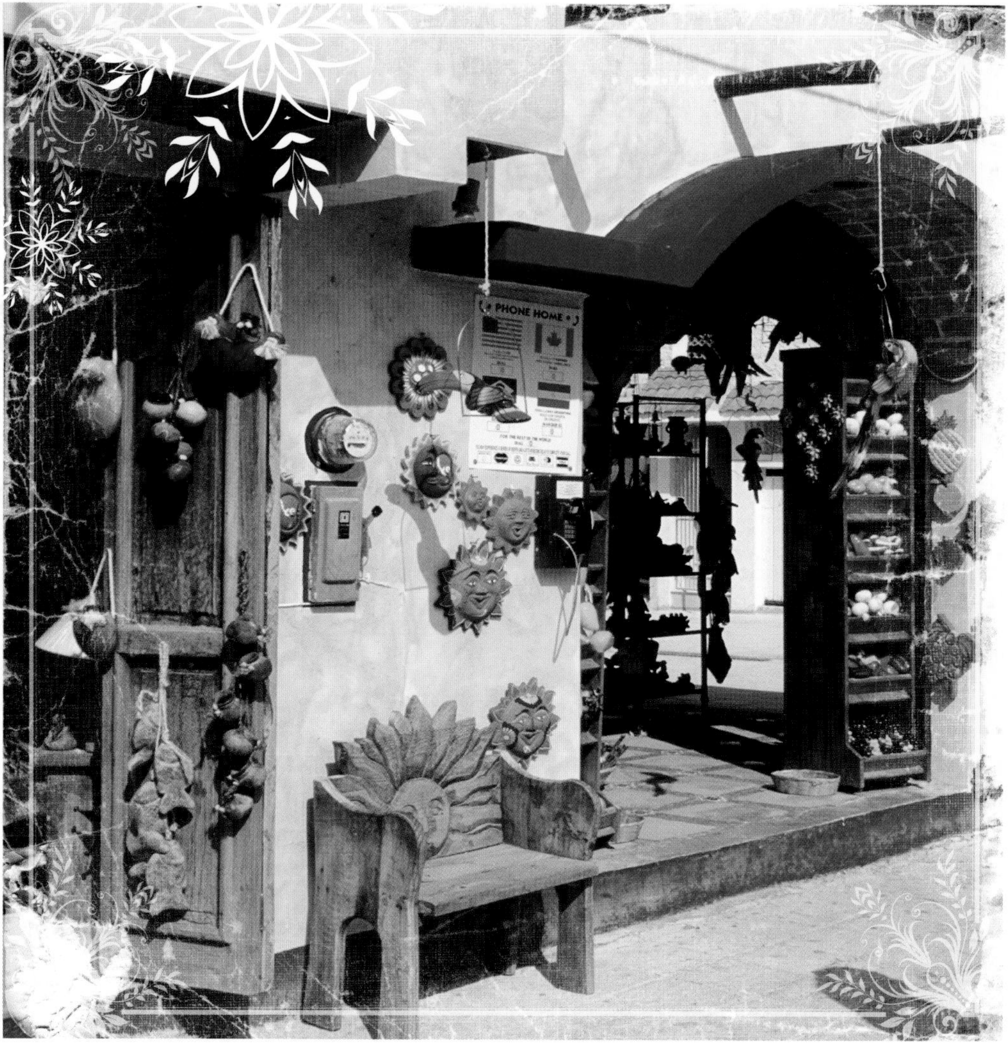
PHONE HOME

❧❦❧

"It would have been a beautiful wedding," Claire retorted, red hair disheveled, "if you hadn't glowered through the whole thing. And it would have been a wonderful honeymoon if we had gone to Aspen or Vail like I wanted."

With a curse, Damon threw his suitcase on the bed, opened it, and began throwing in his clothes. "Let's go home," he said. "At least, I'm going. You can do whatever you want."

But, of course, it was still a long time until their evening flight. When the rain paused in mid-afternoon, it seemed advisable to escape their close quarters. Barely civil, they left the hotel and wandered through the bazaars and markets, inspecting baskets, bowls, carpets, and carvings, looking for just the right item to take home as a souvenir. "Like, maybe, a machete from the rain forest," muttered Damon. But as everything triggered an argument, they were ready to give up when they heard an eager . . .

"Buenos días, señor and *señora."*

They turned to see a small, dark-skinned man, wearing an apron and flashing a bone-white smile.

"Enter into the shop of Felipe Chavez, *por favor*. Look at my carvings. They are very beautiful. I make you good price."

It was his countenance that drew them through the beads and into his shop. But Felipe's smile dimmed as he glanced at their faces. "Ah, *señor* and *señora*," he said, "I do not know many things, but one thing, I know the faces. I can read the lines in the brow, and the mouths and the cheeks and the chins. I can read eyes. And I see an unhappy story, no? Felipe Chavez, he does not like unhappy stories. He likes the ones that are happy ever after, no?"

Damon and Claire glanced at each other, shifted their weight, and shrugged. "We haven't felt well," mumbled Damon.

"No," said Claire. "Damon got sun-burned, and I've been a little . . . uh, sick."

"Oh," said Felipe, "you perhaps had the orange juice at Hotel Presidente? Ah, well," he said, smile returning. "No problem. It is past. Now, *por favor*, look at my carvings. They are works of art. You will find nowhere on the island their equals. They should be in the National Museum, but, alas, I am undiscovered. I make you good price. *Comprende*?"

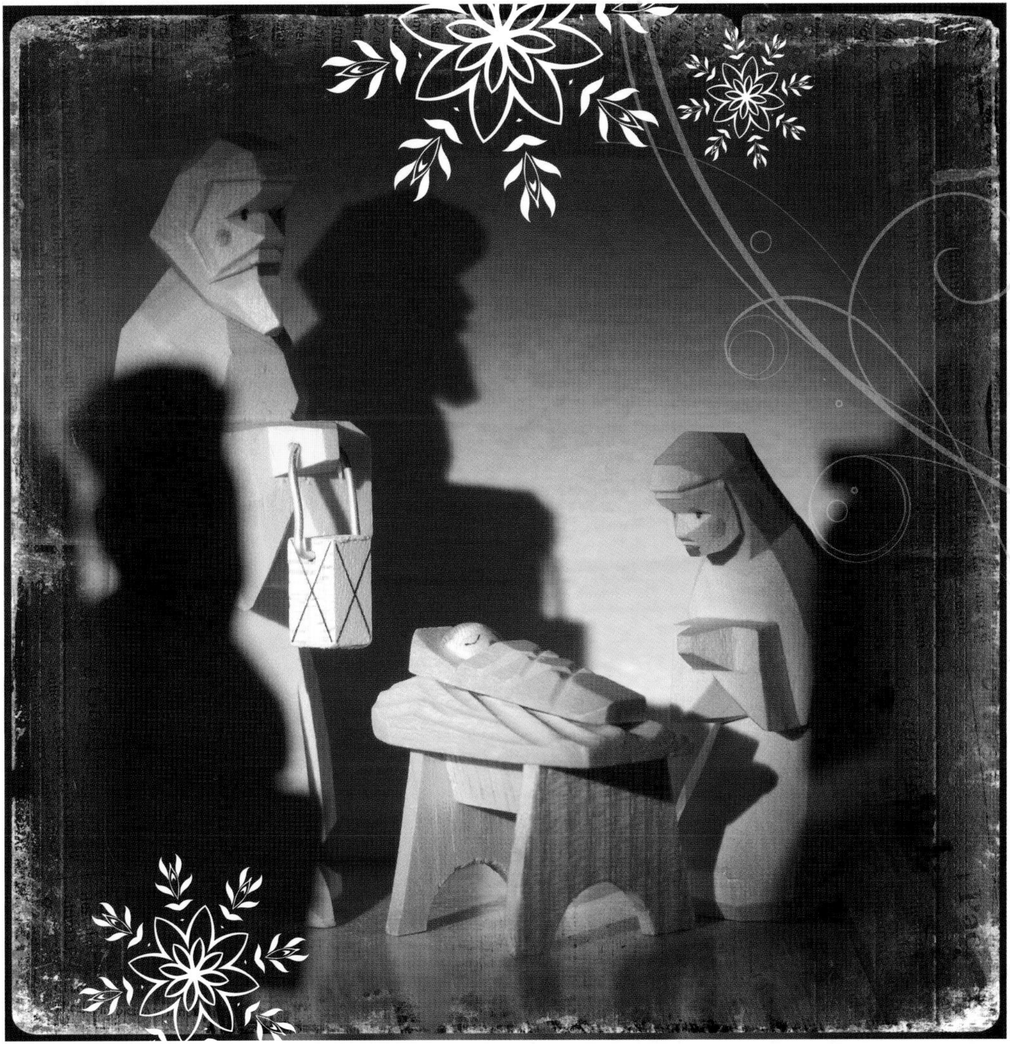

Claire and Damon began exploring the little shop. It was drab and dusty. As they moved from one shelf to another, Felipe followed them like a beggar, switching little spotlights on and off as needed, explaining the distinctive features of each piece.

The figures were all carved from lightly colored wood, and most were about ten inches tall. The bodies were rough hewn, but the faces were exquisite—all of them smiling. There were bullfighters and firefighters, Incas and Indians. All smiling. Even the Spanish conquistadors were smiling. There were stallions and eagles, soccer stars and saints. And all were smiling.

"Your characters," said Claire, "they have such happy faces."

"Ah, *bien*, you have noticed," said Filipe. "I told you. I read faces; that is my hobby. As I work by the window, I watch people passing by. They come, they go, they do not know that Felipe watches them. And when I see a smile, I quickly chisel it onto one of my figures. All these smiles in my shop, they once belonged to people."

As Damon and Claire continued browsing the little, unswept shop, they both saw it at once, a nativity set, displayed by itself at the end of a shelf.

"Oh," said Claire, "I've never seen a crèche like this. Everyone is smiling. Look, the angels seem so happy, and the shepherds. Even Joseph and Mary have smiles. And, oh, look! The Christ child, he is smiling too."

"Of course," Felipe replied. "Why not? It is *Feliz Navidad*—Happy Christmas. Tidings of joy to the world. Lord Jesus, He, only, gives joy *grandé*."

Then Felipe added quietly, "Lord Jesus, he would bring joy *grandé* to you."

"We'll take him," said Damon.

"You'll take Lord Jesus?" asked Felipe.

"Yes," said Claire, "the whole set—Mary, Joseph, the shepherds, and maybe a few extra sheep."

"*Sí, señora*. I will wrap them. It is eighty dollars."

As Damon pulled out a hundred dollar bill, another customer entered the shop. Felipe became distracted, making change and boxing the crèche, while scurrying around, turning tiny spotlights on and off, and hoping for another sale.

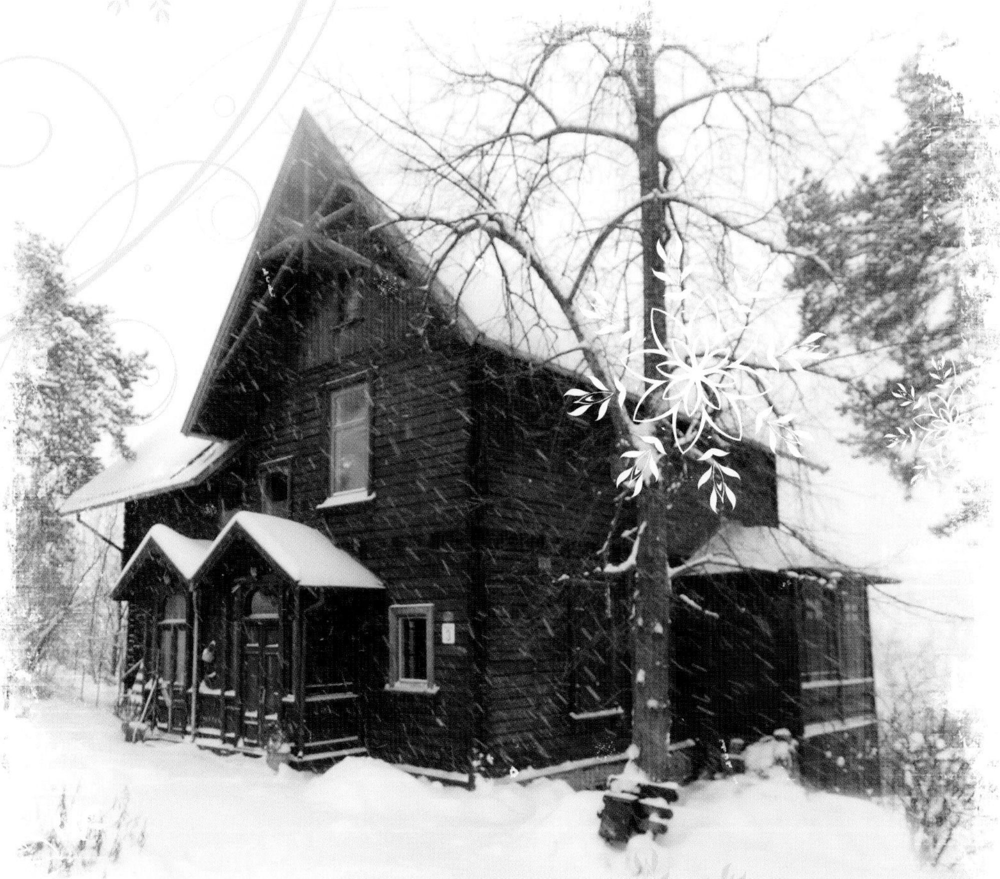

As Claire and Damon strolled to the hotel, they almost felt like newlyweds after all. But the euphoria was short-lived, for the ensuing rush to the airport and dash to their plane soured their spirits again. The flight was crowded and hot, and they returned home with foul moods.

Things grew even worse when they opened their souvenir only to discover that in his haste, Felipe had failed to put the Christ child into the box. The holy parents were there, the angel, the shepherd, and his flock. But Jesus was missing.

Claire began crying as she arranged the pieces on the mantle. Without the Christ child, the crèche seemed hollow and hostile. Even the smiles on the figures lost their charm.

"It's a parable," Damon said grimly. "Our marriage is a mess, God doesn't care, and I don't know what to do about it."

For a week neither spoke much, nor was there much tenderness or intimacy between them. Damon seemed lost in thought. Claire chatted every day with her mother and went about Christmas shopping. But she, too, pondered their future.

On Christmas morning a fresh layer of snow covered the Rockies. The sun was bright, and the air as clear. Claire woke first, and when Damon stirred an hour later, he found her sitting by the tree with the animated eyes of a child, fingering her presents. Christmas music was softly playing. Gathering a blanket around him, Damon joined her cross-legged on the floor.

"Open mine first," Claire eagerly said.

"No, you open mine first."

"No, mine."

"Well, all right," said Damon. "I will. It's so small and thin, I can't imagine what it is." Tearing away the paper, he opened a small, flat box, discovering inside an envelope. It contained a card that looked very much like a wedding invitation. It read: "This is to invite the bearer to a small, private wedding to be held in the snow by the old pine tree on the north side of Stone Church, December 25th, three o'clock."

"I don't understand," said Damon.

Claire looked at him, eyes glistening. "I guess you could say it's a proposal," she said. "I want to start our marriage over again. I called Pastor Humphry about it. He's agreed to let us renew our vows this afternoon. No parents. No photographers. No fancy clothes—just you and me and Pastor."

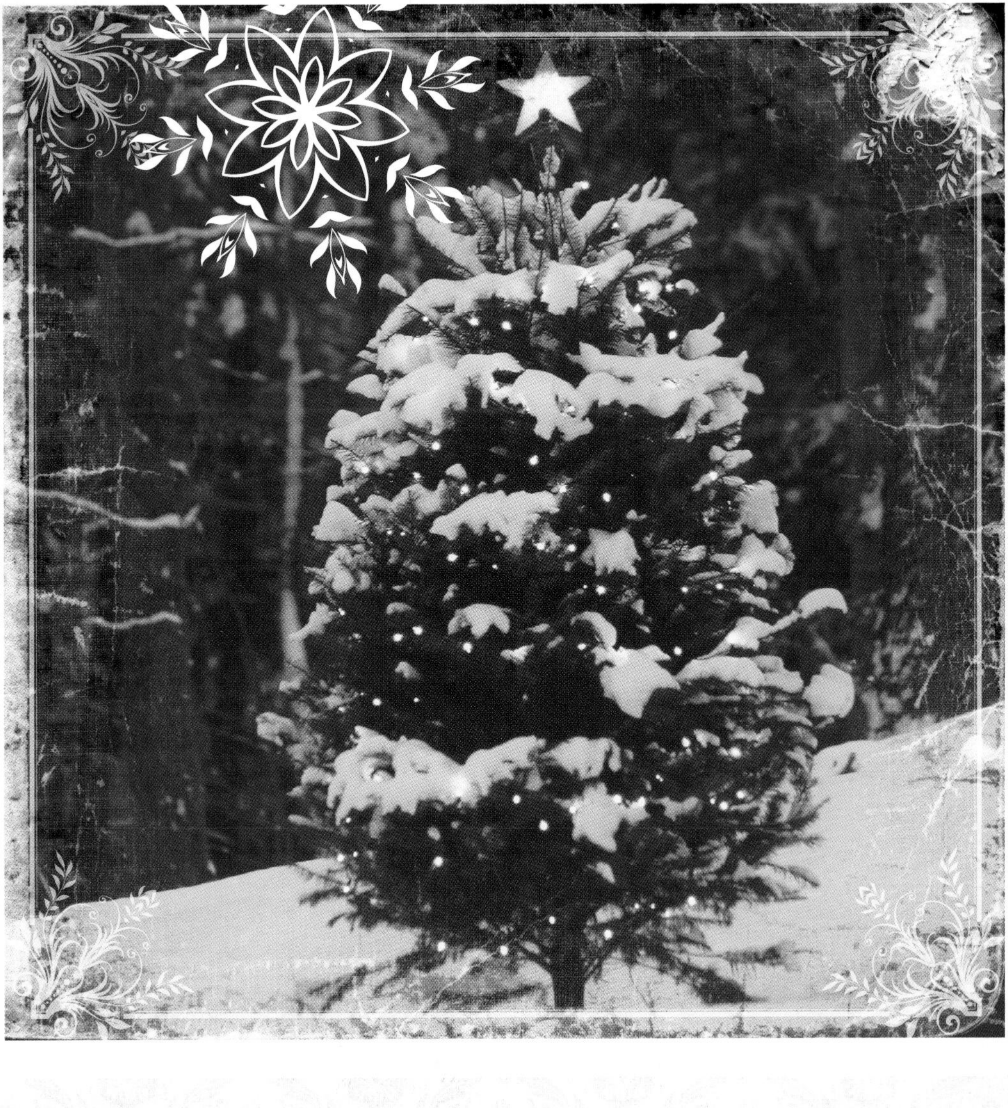

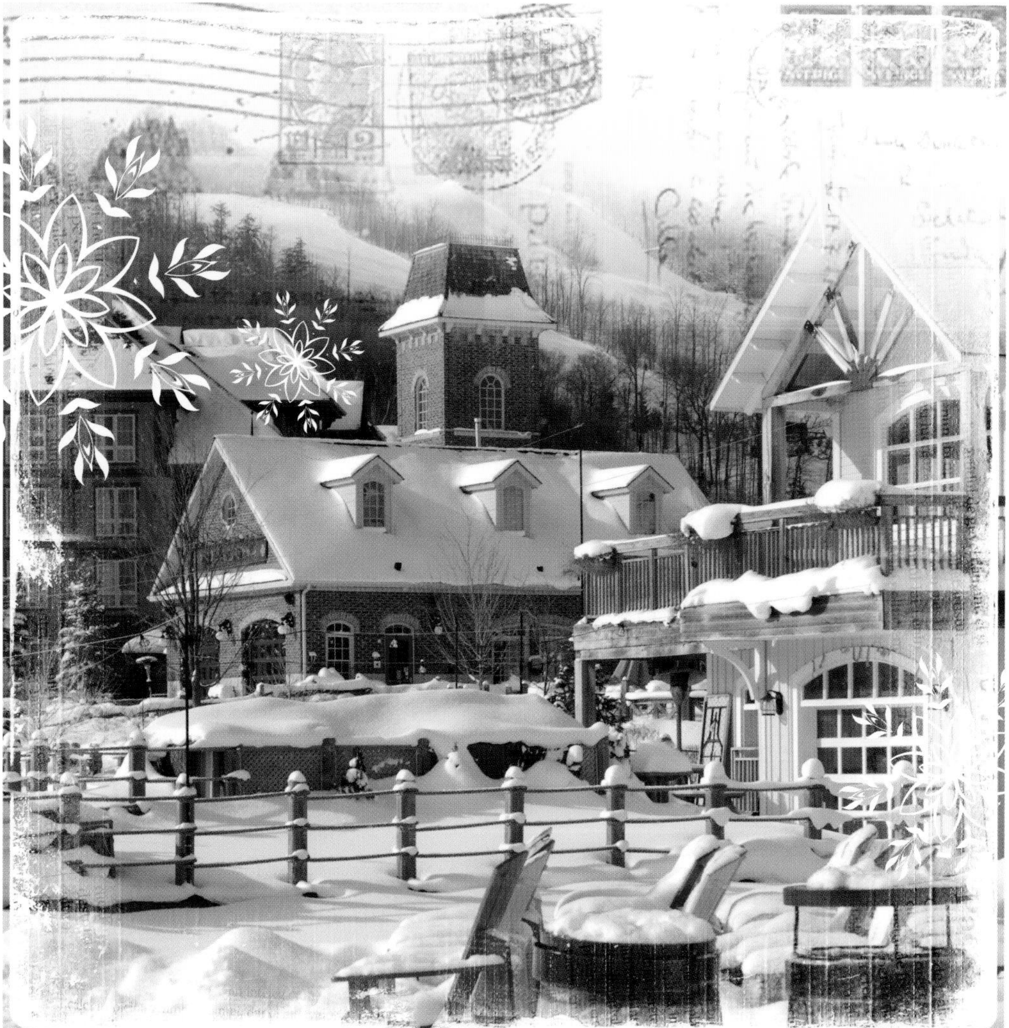

Claire thought she had anticipated Damon's every possible response, but she wasn't prepared when he started chuckling and shaking his head. "What's so funny?" she asked. "What is so funny about that?"

"It's not really funny," said Damon. "It's just that . . . I, uh . . . well . . . here! You open my gift."

Damon held out his gift—equally small and flat—and watched her open it. Inside was a postcard of a little village nestled at the foot of the Rockies.

"I thought we could use a few days in Aspen," said Damon. "Our reservations start tomorrow. I guess . . . well, we can pack for our honeymoon right after our wedding. Isn't that the way it's supposed to work?"

Claire was speechless.

"I felt we needed a new start too," Damon explained. "It's never too soon for a second honeymoon—and never too late. We've got to believe that."

"I do believe it," said Claire, tears coming. "Especially at Christmas. Do you remember what Felipe Chavez said? 'Lord Jesus, He, only, gives joy *grandé*.'"

"Speaking of Felipe Chavez," said Damon, a new tone in his voice, "I'd almost forgotten. It came in yesterday's mail."

Reaching behind the tree, he drew out a small package wrapped in brown paper and bearing special delivery stamps. A wonderment filled Claire's face. She ran for scissors, cut the string, and slit open the box. Inside was a note:

I found this after you left. So sorry. The clerk at the Hotel Presidente is my cousin, and he gave me your address so I hope it arrives by Christmas.

Felipe Chavez

Damon and Claire drew from the box the baby Jesus and carefully restored him to his rightful place on the mantle.

"It's a parable," said Claire.

Damon nodded. "*Feliz Navidad, señora!*" he said, wrapping his arms and his blanket around her. "Or should I say, *Felipe Navidad!*"

And if only Felipe Chavez could have seen them then, he would have carved happy faces all day long.

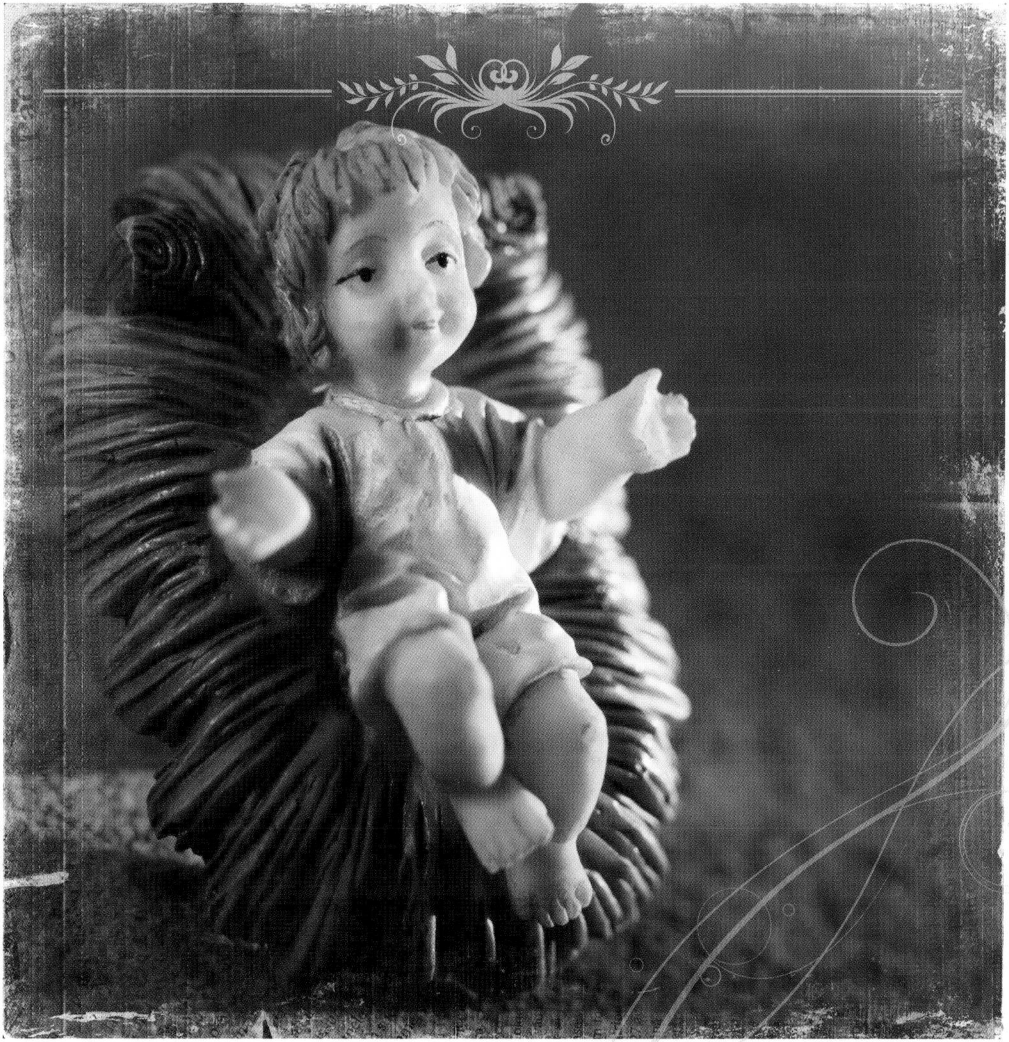

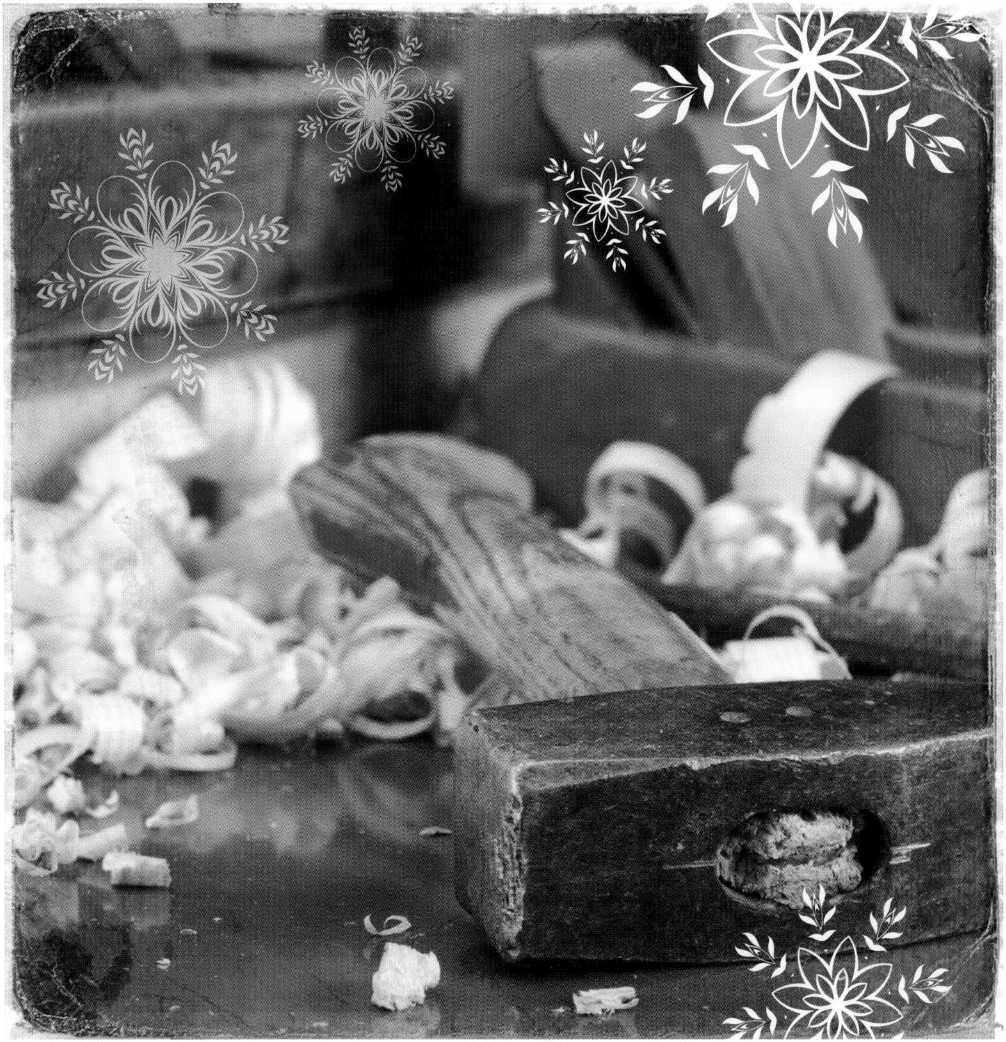

Sugarplum and the Christmas Cradle

 ost of the twists and turns of life can never be anticipated, and few things work out as planned. Even a simple task like building a cradle can be as unpredictable as driving on a rainy night without wipers. This is one such story—a tale of a cradle lovingly made, but never used, and of a baby lovingly conceived, but star-crossed in birth.

The initial news created something of a stir. Some couples wait a while before having children, but not J.B. and Sugarplum. They'd no sooner put their wedding gifts away in the cupboard than they started working on the nursery. News of their love child set tongues a'wagging, and the in-laws were none too pleased.

"You're too immature to have kids," said J.B.'s mother. "Why not wait a couple of years? I'm too young to be a grandma."

J.B. just smirked and said nothing.

Sugarplum did the same when Uncle Adam said bluntly, "This is too soon. You've not been together long enough." The mother-to-be simply patted her stomach and quipped, with a mischievous smile, "It's too late now!"

Down at the work site where the construction of a new building was underway, J.B. took a lot of ribbing from his buddies. "You sure didn't waste any time," said one. "How long you been hitched?"

"Why wait?" said J.B. with a crescent moon smile.

"When's the kid due?"

"In January or February, we'll find out soon. We can hardly wait for him to get here."

"Oh," cackled the men, "so it's already a *him*!"

The young couple, in their joy, took no offense, harbored no anger, and absorbed all the kidding with enviable grace. Soon family and friends were immersed in planning showers, choosing names, making blankets, and stockpiling diapers.

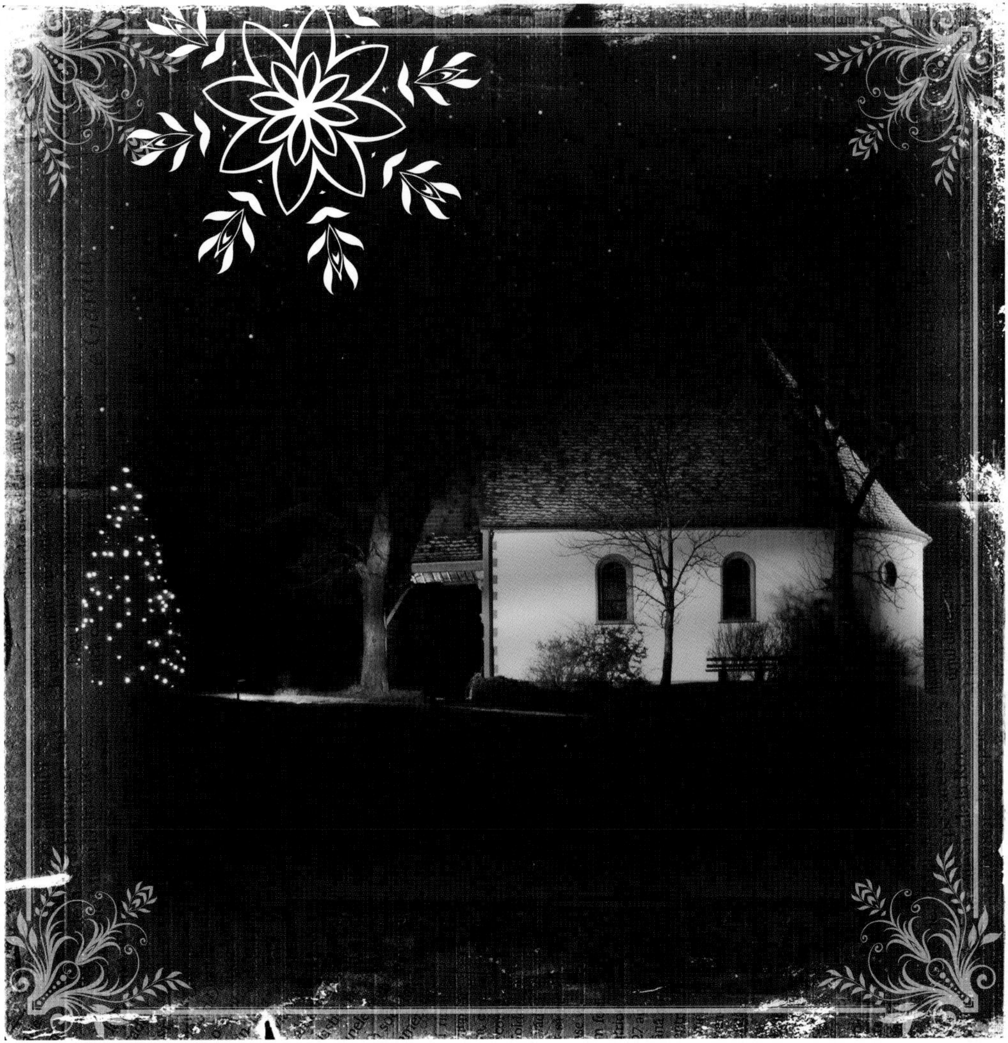

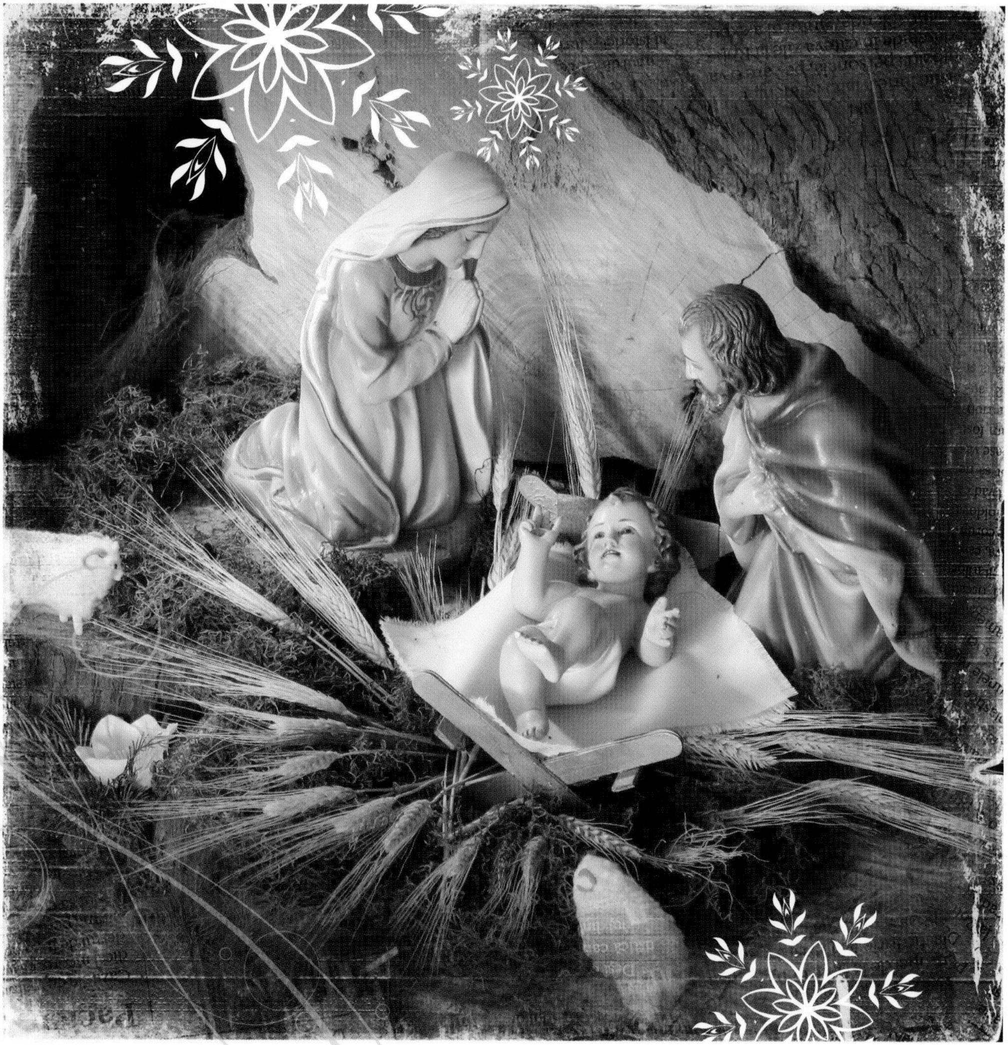

❧

J.B. was certifiably the world's most excited father-to-be, but that wasn't the bad part. The sickening thing was how he treated Sugarplum—not how *badly* he treated her, but how *good* he was to her—like a lethal tonic of molasses.

Sugarplum, don't you think you'd better rest a while?

*Sugarplum, you lie down
while I do the dishes.*

*Sugarplum, you just prop up those twinkle toes and let me rub
your feet.*

Sugarplum was currently his favorite moniker for his brown-eyed wife. During their courtship, he'd called her Babes, but that didn't seem to fit. So he went through a series of other babyish names, like Baby Cakes, Baby Doll, Babe-o-mine, and Babylicious, but none had stuck. So he went on to the C's: Cuddles, Cupcake, Cupid, and Cutie. Later it was Precious, Princess, Pumpkin, and Puffins.

Finally he'd gotten to the S's, and that's when he'd found Sugarplum, and now she was Sugarplum morning, noon, and night. Truth be told, it was getting a little sickening, even to Sugarplum, who felt she was being sugar-pummeled to death.

Sugarplum, let me sweep the floor. I'll go to the market. Let me lift that pot. I'll make the bed. Let me do it.

She put up with it for weeks—it had been so much worse since the start of her pregnancy—but the final straw broke when she doubled over with nausea and vomiting, and J.B. hovered over her like a first-year medical student.

Sugarplum, I can't stand to see you like this, with this awful morning sickness. I think that if you have to throw up, I'll just throw up too.

And he actually did!

That's when she put her foot down. "J.B.," she declared, "I love you, but you are driving me crazy. You've got to find something to do around here besides following me around morning and night. You need an outlet for your energy."

"But, Sugarplum . . ."

"That's enough *Sugarplumming* for now. Find something useful to do while I finish supper—and make sure it's out of my sight! Why not clean out the workshop? I'll call you when the lamb chops are done."

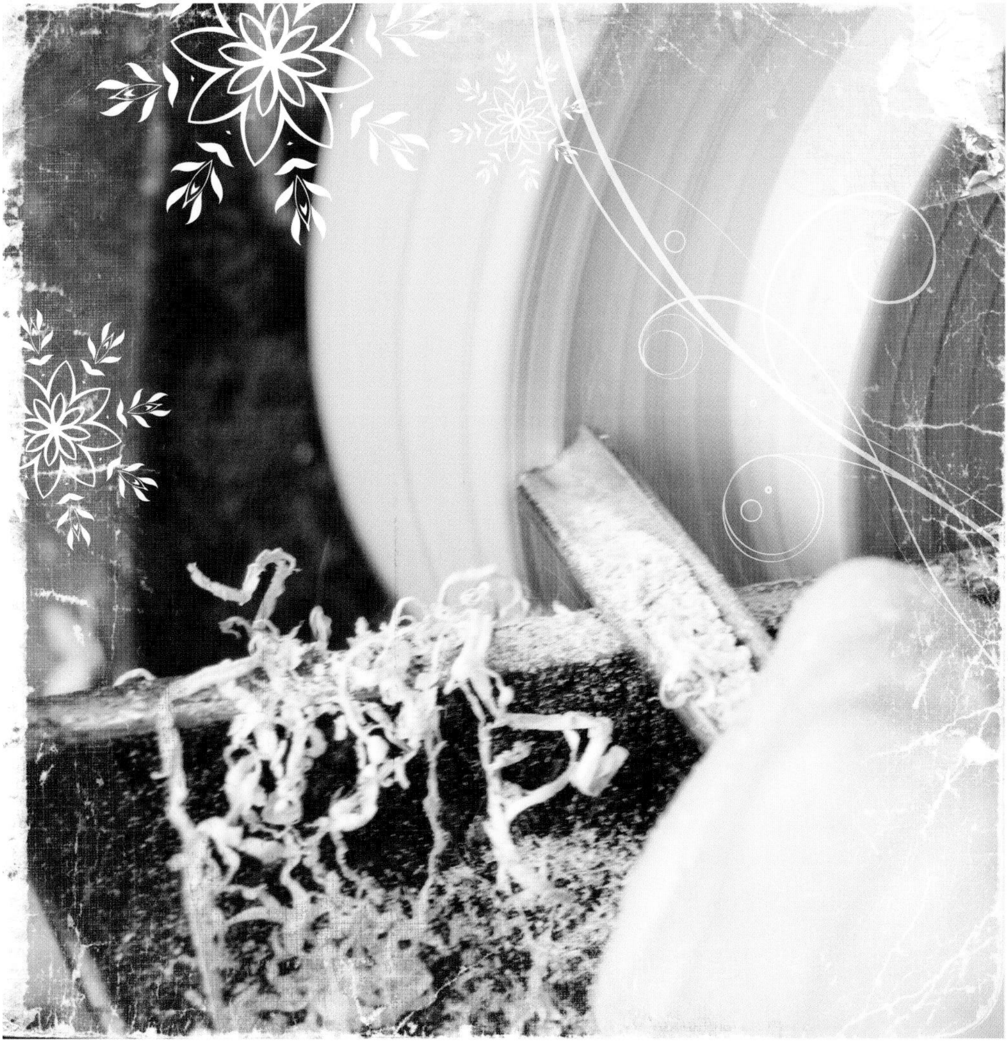

And that's how J.B. started working on that ominous cradle. He meandered to the garage, shifted around some boxes, found an oak plank, and the idea came to him in a flash of inspiration. Yes, it should be oak and not pine, because this wasn't a job for a soft wood. This cradle would be molded from beautiful hardwood with rich grain patterns and unique designs. His creativity went into high gear, and before supper the entire project had come together in his mind. Even for a woodworker like J.B., a cradle is a challenge to build. It's one thing to have the skills and tools to do the job; it's another thing to know how to design furniture and have the knowledge of construction techniques required for the task.

Of course, J.B. could have ordered a set of plans, but he wanted this cradle to be one-of-a-kind, because it was for his one-of-a-kind child. For the next several days, Sugarplum found herself blissfully neglected as J.B. spent every spare moment before and after work at the kitchen table, sketching, erasing, drawing, and designing the project. It was to be a very traditional cradle—not one that hangs on a frame and swings like a pendulum, but an open trough that sits low on the floor, with rockers on either end, and a wooden covering rising at one end as a canopy for the baby's head. No spindles to trap the baby's arms or legs, but a closed-in, tiny sanctuary for the little soul.

It had to be deep enough for a small mattress, of course, and big enough for the baby to use for some time. Every edge had to be rounded and smooth, with no rough spots, cracked boards, or splinters. And no nails or screws. Everything would be dovetailed and hand-pegged.

Most important, it had to rock smoothly and gently, but not too much. "Can't have it tipping over when the kid's old enough to stand up in it," said J.B., erasing a line and reducing an angle. After determining the radius for the rockers, he began finalizing his sketches, and soon Sugarplum saw much less of him, to her enormous relief. Before work, after work, and on weekends, he was sawing, chiseling, routing, assembling, and sanding. Along the way he salvaged the scrap pieces of leftover wood, carefully shaping and sanding them into a beautiful set of building blocks. But most of his attention was on the cradle.

"I've got to get it done in plenty of time," he told his buddies down at the construction site. "I've found a nontoxic finish, but the stain has to dry for about a month so there's no danger of the little fellow getting any fumes. Of course, he might come early, so I need have the whole thing finished by late November."

By now, Sugarplum was starting to miss her man, and she was relieved when he reentered her life full force. After all, she was great with child, as they say, and for the first time, she really did need his help.

"I feel like you've been away on a trip," she told him.

"Well, just you wait till you see it. It's been a labor of love," he said. "It's for you as much as for our kid. You know what they say: 'The hand that rocks the cradle rules the world.' Besides, with all the children we're gonna have, that cradle will have a long career. Then the grandkids will use it, and the great-grandchildren. I feel like I've created an heirloom, a masterpiece."

"Well, are you going to keep on talking about it," asked Sugarplum, "or are you going to let me see it?"

Fetching a dishtowel from the kitchen, J.B. covered Sugarplum's eyes and led her into the nursery. When he removed the rag, there it was—a cradle so beautifully designed, so stunning in its simplicity, that Sugarplum wept the moment she saw it. The grain patterns of the wood were enhanced by the rich oaken colors of the dark stain, and the rockers were so smooth and perfectly aligned that it practically rocked itself. A little galaxy of six-pointed stars was painted onto the end of the cradle, but otherwise it was unadorned. A golden blanket was folded over the mattress, compliments of J.B.'s mother who was a gifted seamstress.

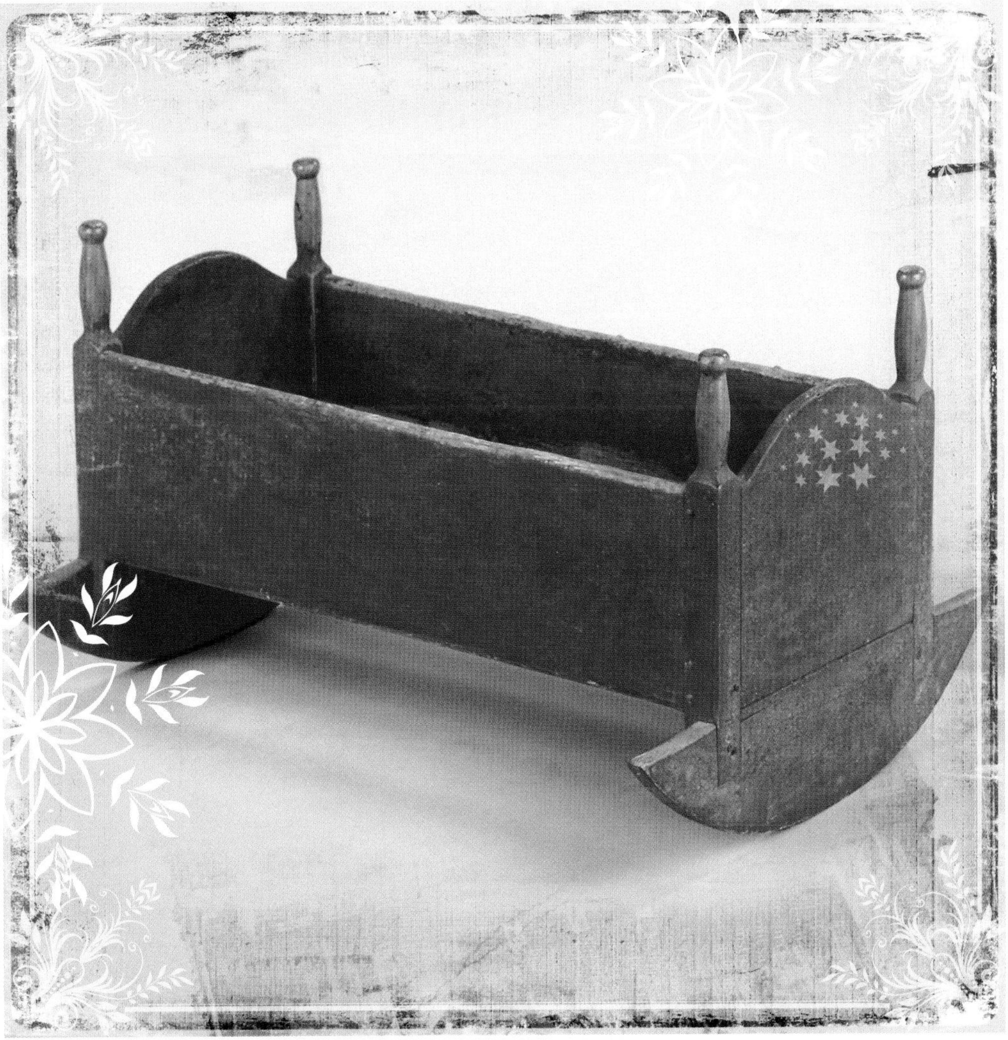

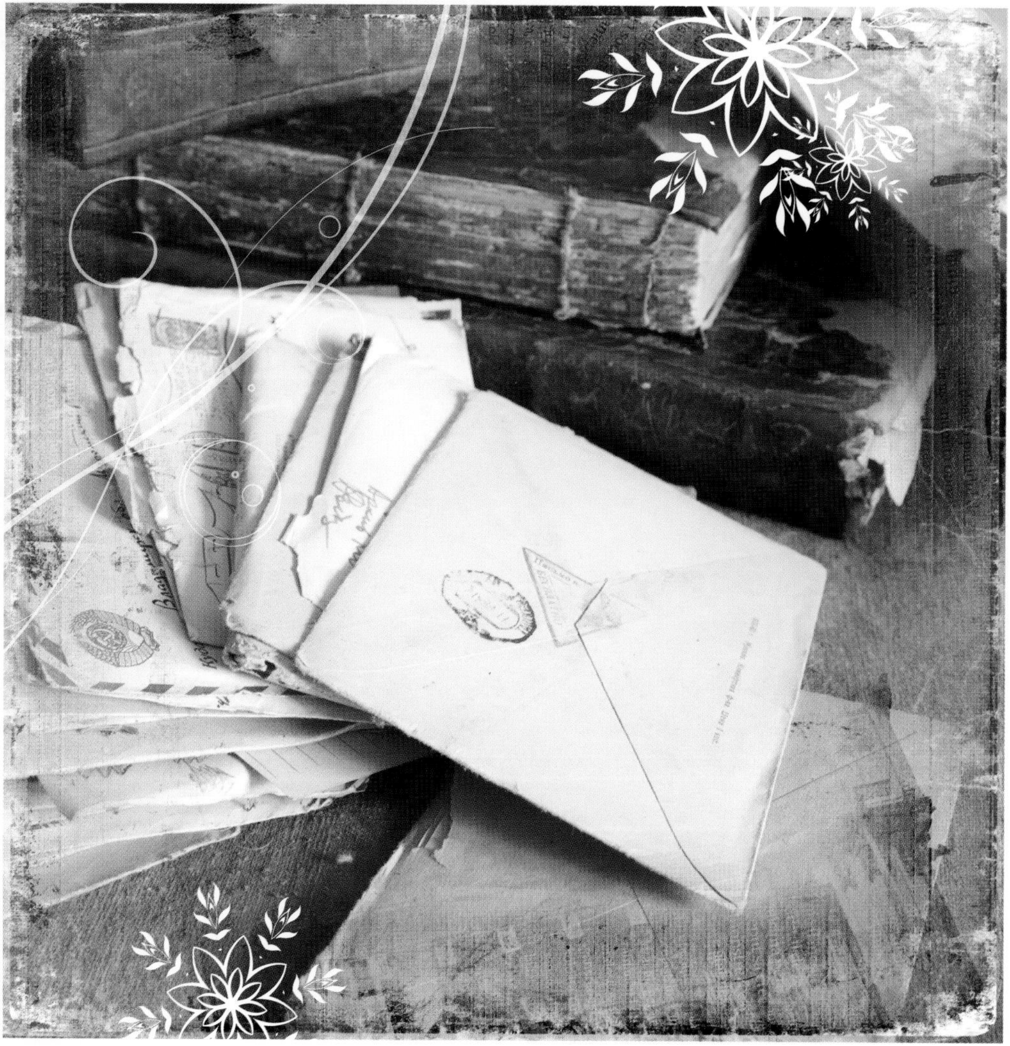

Sugarplum sat on a stool beside the little bed and caressed it, running her hand across the rich lumber. In her mind's eye, she could see her little one sleeping peacefully within its secure walls. J.B. knelt beside her, and it seemed natural for them to ask God to bless the tiny baby whose birthday was only weeks away. The palm of J.B.'s rough hand gently rested against Sugarplum's stomach and, right on cue, he felt the baby move as though already part of the family—which, of course, he was.

It was the calm before the storm. As it happened, for all the work that went into it, the cradle was never used and their little fellow never laid his head within its enclosure. The nursery remained empty, the tiny house was vacated, and the young couple's lives were traumatized.

The culprit was a registered letter that arrived at bedtime, addressed to one Joseph ben Jacob, ordering him to Bethlehem as part of a national census. Against all advice, Sugarplum went with him, mounted on the family donkey.

So it was, that while they were there, the days were completed for her to be delivered. And she brought forth her firstborn Son, and wrapped Him in swaddling cloths, and laid Him in a . . . manger.

(Luke 2:6–7)